What is Social Policy?

D0861651

To Angela

What is Social Policy?

Understanding the Welfare State

Daniel Béland

polity

Copyright © Daniel Béland 2010

The right of Daniel Béland to be identified as Author of this Work has been asserted in accordance with the UK Copyright, Designs and Patents Act 1988.

First published in 2010 by Polity Press, reprinted in 2012 (twice), 2013, 2014

Polity Press
65 Bridge Street
Cambridge CB2 1UR, UK

Polity Press
350 Main Street
Malden, MA 02148, USA

All rights reserved. Except for the quotation of short passages for the purpose of criticism and review, no part of this publication may be reproduced, stored in a retrieval system, or transmitted, in any form or by any means, electronic, mechanical, photocopying, recording or otherwise, without the prior permission of the publisher.

ISBN-13: 978-0-7456-4583-4
ISBN-13: 978-0-7456-4584-1 (pb)

A catalogue record for this book is available from the British Library.

Typeset in 11 on 13 pt Sabon
by Servis Filmsetting Ltd, Stockport, Cheshire
Printed and bound by the USA by Edwards Brothers, Inc.

The publisher has used its best endeavours to ensure that the URLs for external websites referred to in this book are correct and active at the time of going to press. However, the publisher has no responsibility for the websites and can make no guarantee that a site will remain live or that the content is or will remain appropriate.

Every effort has been made to trace all copyright holders, but if any have been inadvertently overlooked the publisher will be pleased to include any necessary credits in any subsequent reprint or edition.

For further information on Polity, visit our website: www.politybooks.com

Contents

List of Tables

Preface & Acknowledgements

What is social policy? Why do we have large social programs, and why are some of them politically controversial? How do these programs affect individuals and families? How and why are American social programs different from the ones available in other developed nations? What is the future of the welfare state, exactly? Finally, why does it matter to you? These are the questions at the center of this short political sociology book, which is grounded in a comparative perspective while focusing on the United States.

I wrote this book because I wanted to share some basic ideas about social policy with a broader audience than the people who typically read journal articles and research monographs. Social policy is a complex field, but this book had to be very concise, which means that I only surveyed a limited number of relevant issues. I did my best, however, to cover some of the major social policy debates of our time in order to help people grasp the "big picture." No survey is ever complete, but I spent much time exploring issues about which I felt readers may want to know. Readers familiar with my other publications will recognize some of my favorite themes and examples; nevertheless, I have also addressed many new problems I find essential for readers to know about. This is a scholarly overview, but I hope that it is accessible enough to help many different people think about important social policy issues.

Many people helped me write this book. First, I would like

to thank the people who commented on previous drafts of the manuscript: Kurtis Balon, Jeremy Busch-Howell, Larry DeWitt, Michael Kpessa, David McGrane, John Myles, Tasleem Padamsee, and the anonymous reviewers. Over the years, I have collaborated with many different scholars. Thank you to all of them for the support and the intellectual stimulation: Kristina Babich, Edward D. Berkowitz, Julia Brotea, David Chinitz, Robert H. Cox, Larry DeWitt, Brian Gran, Jacob Hacker, Randall Hansen, Christopher Howard, Julie Kaye, Michael Kpessa, André Lecours, Rianne Mahon, Patrik Marier, Kimberly Morgan, John Myles, Mitchell Orenstein, Heather Rollwagen, Toshimitsu Shinkawa, François Vergniolle de Chantal, Jean-Philippe Viriot Durandal, Alex Waddan, Colin Wiseman, Ka Man Yu, Mike Zajko, and Claudia Zamorano. Special thanks to Ann Orloff for her insight about gender research. Thank you to my colleagues and students at the Johnson-Shoyama School for their intellectual stimulation. I also want to thank Justin Dyer and Geri Rowlatt for their copy-editing assistance, as well as the Canada Research Chairs Program for its support. At Polity Press, Emma Longstaff and Jonathan Skerrett provided guidance and useful suggestions at different stages of the editorial process: many thanks for the advice and for the opportunity to publish in this excellent series. Finally, I would like to thank my wife Angela, who has loved and supported me for more than ten years. Because she is so smart, brave, and patient, I dedicate this book to her!

Introduction

From health-care to unemployment insurance and old-age pensions, the welfare state is a significant aspect of our lives. For instance, when a major recession hit the United States in 2008, millions of Americans realized how unemployment benefits are important to helping people bounce back after they lose their job. Moreover, when they grow old, most citizens are glad that they can count on programs like Medicare and Social Security. Not only are we all likely to depend on a social program at some point in our existence but, as workers and taxpayers, we help finance social programs with our payroll contributions and when we pay income tax. Although economically vulnerable people rely more on social programs than better-off citizens do, social policy is not just for the poor (Rosner 2003:3). In the United States, the vast majority of elderly people, even wealthier ones, receive Social Security benefits. Beyond public social programs like Social Security, private benefits also play a major role in social policy. This is especially true in the United States, where private health insurance and old-age pensions are widespread but unequally distributed. Interestingly, even such private schemes are related to state action,[1] because tax incentives and regulations shape their development. But social policy is not simply about the state; major civil-society actors, ranging from business organizations and religious groups to labor unions and women's groups, are involved in social policy debates. And, even if these policy debates may sound overly technical, they generally raise major political and social

1

issues like the enduring nature of class, gender, and racial inequalities. This is what makes social policy, as a field, an intriguing lens through which we can analyze key social trends and political struggles – and the historical forces underpinning them. Knowing about the long history of modern social programs in the United States, and elsewhere, is necessary for understanding why we have our current social programs and how those programs could evolve over the next few decades. Social policy is both a controversial topic and a fragmented landscape, and every citizen should know how it works, why it is there, and why they should care. At the broadest level, this is what you will learn from this book.

What is This Book About?

This book is a concise political and sociological introduction to social policy, one that takes both a comparative and a historical perspective on the American welfare state.[2] To understand what is going on in the United States, it is necessary to know about social programs in general and about the experience of other countries in particular. This is true for two main reasons. First, because developed countries face the same basic economic, social, and political challenges, we need the "big picture" in mind to grasp how they respond to these challenges by making specific political choices. At a time when globalization is such a significant issue, this "big picture" is necessarily international in nature. Second, comparing the United States with other countries that share a similar level of economic development is crucial for recognizing what is both common and unique to the modern American welfare state. There is a great deal of talk about "American exceptionalism," but only a comparative and an international approach can help locate the United States within the contemporary developed world, and put into perspective the policy choices made in that country. In short, this book was written to help you better understand the nature of the welfare state and what is specific about the United States in terms of its social programs and the political struggles over them.

Before going any further, it is worth noting what this book is *not* about. First, it is not a detailed description of the major social programs that exist today in the United States and in other developed nations: for example, it does not enumerate policy details that are easily available on government websites. Yet, in order to understand the politics of the welfare state, we need to know how social programs work and how some of their key characteristics can affect the social and political mobilizations surrounding them. Second, it is not a detailed study of the history of the American welfare state. Many books are available on this topic, including those devoted to specific issues and programs such as Medicare, Social Security, and welfare reform (e.g., Achenbaum 1986; Berkowitz 1991; Oberlander 2003; Quadagno 1994). Drawing on this scholarship, this book simply attempts to help you grasp some of the major moments in the political history of the American welfare state, which is full of interesting twists and turns. Finally, it is not a look at the future of social policy that tells you what should be done and what is right or wrong. Obviously, no author is truly "neutral" and, when writing about the historical and political fate of social programs, I have an opinion about the core policy issues addressed in this book. For instance, I believe that the state must play a major role in society, something that libertarians object to. But, although my book is not devoid of policy opinions, no bold political stance on the issues of the day has been taken.

After reading this book, you will probably have a better idea about how the welfare state and the political battles over it take shape, which, in turn, can help you take a more enlightened stance in today's debates on the future of social policy in the United States and around the world. Perhaps as important, you will also learn how social scientists, especially sociologists and political scientists, analyze welfare state politics. Good research on social policy is not purely technical. Going well beyond the description of how programs operate, it enhances our knowledge of the social and political forces that shape our world. This is another way to say that good social policy research is good social science research. The goal of this book is to help you increase your understanding of how politics, especially the struggles over citizenship, inequality, and redistribution, impacts our lives. More specifically, this book is about helping you understand why national welfare states are different from one another, and how it can and does matter every day for millions and millions of people.

Overview

At heart, this book is a sociological and political introduction to social policy, but it does put forward a number of claims about the nature of social programs and the theories of welfare state development and restructuring. To stress the most important of these claims, and to keep the "big picture" in mind, what follows is a concise, chapter-by-chapter overview of the book, which should help map the complex issues raised throughout it.

The first thing to know about social policy is the various roles social programs can play in society. Why social policy, exactly? The first chapter begins by addressing this question, the answer to which is not as simple as you might think. Instead of having only one goal, social programs can simultaneously pursue several objectives, such as fighting poverty, reinforcing citizenship through inequality reduction, and emancipating workers and citizens from market dependency. To add to this plurality of policy goals, there are different types of social programs that operate according to distinct fiscal and political logics. For instance, a substantial gap exists between targeted social assistance programs for the poor and social insurance programs that cover the vast majority of the population. Finally, because the term "social policy" refers to programs ranging from health-care services to unemployment benefits and old-age pensions, the objectives and nature of social programs vary significantly from one policy area to another. As argued in Chapter 1, understanding key differences between policy areas is a major task of social policy research; so, even before we start comparing countries, we must recognize the diversity of programs and policy areas that often exist within the same country.

Once major policy goals, types of programs, and policy areas have been mapped, it is much easier to assess the systematic comparative and international perspectives available to identify what is specific about the American welfare state. In the world of social policy, as elsewhere, being aware of the prevailing situation in other countries is the best way to recognize what is common and what is really specific about your country. An interesting analytical device for mapping the international social policy landscape is the concept of welfare regime, which is discussed in Chapter 2. Although this device can be misleading, when used with caution it remains a useful tool for identifying broad country clusters. For example, knowing that the United States is the best example of the "liberal welfare regime" leads us to other countries associated with this cluster, especially the United Kingdom and Canada. In policy areas such as old-age pensions, these three countries share an extensive reliance on private social benefits, a key aspect of social policy debates in the United States. This is why, in the second section of Chapter 2, the fragmentation of these private benefits and the indirect fiscal and regulatory roles of the state in this area are discussed at length. Paradoxically, because the state plays such a dominant role in setting and overseeing the development of private social benefits, these benefits are seldom purely "private."

Overall, the discussion on welfare regimes and private benefits stresses the relationship between inequality and social policy, a relationship that is not only about class but also about gender, race, and ethnicity. For instance, in the United States, in a context of historically rooted patterns of discrimination and inequality, African-Americans and Hispanics are typically less affluent and more vulnerable economically than the average population, which has crucial social policy consequences, especially because the welfare state can both reflect and challenge existing social inequalities. In fact, variations from one country to another, and even from one policy area to another in the same country, are tied to enduring patterns of inequality that social programs either challenge or reinforce, depending on the policy choices that are made.

In the last section of Chapter 2, the argument is made that key institutional differences between countries in the territorial organization of the welfare state can have a strong impact on the politics of social policy, which partially reflects the geographical distribution of inequalities. Recognizing that both inequalities and social programs have significant territorial implications is especially critical for analyzing the politics of the welfare state in a federal country such as the United States. Yet, saying that the United States is a federal country does not mean much from a comparative standpoint, as the nature of federal institutions is unique to each federal system. As evidenced here and in other chapters, comparing the United States with its federal neighbor Canada is particularly useful for identifying some of the original features of the American welfare state. Other scholars have demonstrated interest in the Canadian experience for the comparative study of "American exceptionalism" (Banting, Hoberg, and Simeon 1997; Boychuk 2008; Lipset 1990; Maioni 1998; Théret, 1999), and this book simply follows their path.

Taking a comparative approach to the welfare state is necessary. But, to grasp the politics of social policy and today's social challenges, it is not enough to just compare the United States to other countries – we need to supplement our comparative analysis with historical research. In the social sciences and social policy research, historical and comparative perspectives are intimately related, especially in the case of sociology and political science (e.g., Amenta, Bonastia, and Caren 2001). More than a century ago, Max Weber (1978; 2003), who is widely recognized as a founder of both disciplines, spelled out the need to take both a historical and a comparative perspective in order to understand the modern world. The welfare state is a major aspect of that world because it is closely related to broad historical and social processes, such as the rise of capitalism and the expansion of the modern state. Furthermore, recent scholarship suggests that it is sometimes impossible to explain major policy developments without paying close attention to the timing and sequence of historical events that have led to the outcome we seek to explain (Pierson 2004). This is yet another reason to recognize that, under many circumstances, the present is difficult to grasp without a profound knowledge of the past. At the same time, it is less about learning a few dates by heart than it is about having the "big picture" in mind while identifying potential causal factors that may have driven the changes we seek to explain. In other words, we can understand better about the past using systematic theories.

Theoretical frameworks are available to explain major differences between countries that took shape over time. Thus, following a brief overview of the history of modern social policy in Europe and the United States, Chapter 3 examines the theories of welfare state development that are used to explain major cross-national differences in the emergence of modern social programs throughout the twentieth century, especially during the three decades of economic prosperity after World War II (1939–45). These theories focus on four sets of factors: economic and demographic change; labor mobilization; political institutions; and culture and ideas. Although described as competing against one another to explain historical and political differences between countries, in some cases available theories of welfare state development complement one another (Myles and Quadagno 2002). This claim is at the center of Chapter 3, which provides you with the basic time-frame and theoretical tools you need to take a genuinely historical and comparative look at welfare state politics in the United States and other developed countries.

Chapter 4 is devoted to welfare state politics during the last three decades, both in the United States and in other developed countries. As far as social programs are concerned, the economic crisis of the mid- to late 1970s and the subsequent election of conservative leaders such as Margaret Thatcher and Ronald Reagan marked the end of an era of unilateral welfare state expansion. What has occurred since then is more complex than some scholars have argued, in large part because cutbacks and expansion have frequently taken place simultaneously. For example, in the United States, the Clinton years witnessed the end of a major entitlement program (Aid to Families with Dependent Children [AFDC]), the expansion of Medicaid, and even the creation of a new program aimed at increasing health insurance coverage for children (the State Children's Health Insurance Program [SCHIP] now known as CHIP). As suggested in Chapter 4, this example is not unique to the United States; other developed countries have seen cutbacks and progressive restructuring take place, either simultaneously or relatively close together. Thus, from an international and comparative perspective, what are the dominant trends in contemporary social policy change? This question is at the center of a debate between those who argue that developed countries are converging toward a common, market-friendly model and those who claim that national differences created during previous historical moments remain strong. Although it is perhaps too early to fully answer the question, Chapter 4 offers a critical overview of the debate on it.

But, you may ask, what about the future? Most social scientists are not good at predicting the future, and this book does not attempt to do that. Instead, Chapter 5 stresses a number of looming issues that are the focus of contemporary debates on the future of the welfare state – issues that may not have always entered mainstream American political discussions in this area but may, at some point, have greater political significance. Mainly, the chapter describes major issues like globalization, growing health-care costs, and rising social inequalities that shape contemporary social policy debates.

Although Chapter 5 and the book as a whole only offer a broad overview of the complex world of social policy, my hope is that, from this, you will gain a better idea of how social programs work, what may explain their development, and what welfare state politics is about. Social programs are a major aspect of our lives as citizens, taxpayers, and workers, and being knowledgeable about these programs is a matter of civic duty and political enlightenment. As evidenced throughout this book, taking a comparative, historical, and political look at social policy is a great way to understand social policy and the welfare state.

1

Social Policy and the Welfare State

At different stages of our life, many of us rely on social programs in one way or another. For example, when we lose our job, we can access unemployment insurance benefits that provide some financial support while we look for a new job. Without these benefits, we could have no other choice but sell our home or perhaps even fall into destitution. During the recession that struck the United States in 2008 and 2009, many people who had never thought they could suddenly lose their job ended up unemployed, and officials scrambled to improve unemployment insurance benefits as millions of Americans struggled to provide for their families during hard times. When the economy is growing, many of us think that we may never need unemployment insurance benefits. When a major economic crisis strikes, however, we suddenly realize that we could be much more vulnerable to a job loss than we had previously thought. Suddenly, we feel lucky that unemployment benefits are available if we need them.

This example perfectly illustrates the vital role of social programs in our lives. But beyond this example, what is social policy, exactly? Related to the development of both capitalism and the modern state, social policy is an institutionalized response to social and economic problems, ranging from economic insecurity to inequality and poverty. Key differences exist between policy areas and between types of social programs. For example, providing adequate income support to retired people is very different from making quality health-care accessible to the population as a whole. Thus, to understand social policy and the welfare state, we should consider the specific characteristics of concrete policy areas and social programs while keeping an eye on the "big picture."

The first section of this chapter conveys the "big picture" concept by discussing several possible understandings of social policy and of the role of the welfare state in developed societies. The second and third sections highlight the diversity of welfare state arrangements by discussing two critical institutional issues: program types and policy areas. The second section explores the principal differences in financing and benefits between three major types of social programs: social assistance; social insurance; and universal transfers and services. The nature of five major social policy areas central to the modern welfare state – work, unemployment, and welfare; pensions; health-care; housing; and family benefits – is discussed in the third section.

Why Social Policy?

There are different ways to study social policy. In some countries, social policy refers both to a set of social programs and to an autonomous field of research and teaching, with its own degrees, departments, and schools. In the United Kingdom, for example, social policy is an interdisciplinary field that bridges disciplines like sociology and political science while remaining distinct from social work, which focuses more on counseling than on policy and administration.[1] In the United States, however, social policy is seldom considered to be an autonomous academic field and, as in other nations, people from disciplines such as economics, political science, sociology, and social work study the role of social programs and explore social policy issues in ways that reflect their disciplinary traditions. For example, when dealing with social policy issues, economists tend to focus on incentives and fiscal constraints, sociologists are more likely to attend to the relationship between social programs and specific forms of inequality, and political scientists often emphasize the impact of political parties and interest groups on welfare state development. However, although the influence of traditional academic disciplines remains high in the United States, it is almost impossible to study the welfare state without drawing on scholarship from a number of subject areas. At the same time, to understand social policy debates, we must constantly be aware of disciplinary boundaries that affect how researchers frame the issues they study. Studying social policy is always about defining the reality in which we are interested, and that is not without arbitrariness.

Beyond these cautionary remarks, how do scholars typically describe the role of social policy? There is no real consensus, but there are a number of possible answers that generally complement one another. Because social policy definitions are easily available in the literature, instead of simply listing them it is much more interesting to consider several possible interpretations of social policy, before bridging them to formulate a new working definition. This also ensures that the possible goals and boundaries of social programs in contemporary societies are clear. For example, it would be a mistake to think that social policy is only about helping the poor. Although scholars like Karl Polanyi (2001) have demonstrated that over the last century in the Anglo-American world, modern social policy emerged from the Elizabethan Poor Law tradition, it has acquired a much broader meaning, one that concerns the population as a whole and not just the poor (Castel 2003). For instance, in most developed countries, public health insurance covers the entire population. In the United States, the push for universal coverage that had been debated for decades was central to the health-care debate that divided citizens and politicians in 2009 and early 2010 (Chapter 5).

More generally, it is important to remember that perceptions of social policy – how it is understood – are grounded in particular assumptions about the nature of capitalism and the relationship between state and society, and that, although these perceptions point to general characteristics of social policy, they may reflect specific national contexts. This observation is especially crucial for North American readers, because several of the most prominent social policy thinkers are European, which is hardly surprising given that the modern welfare state first began to emerge in

11

Europe more than a century ago. Even though welfare state development took a distinct path in the United States (Amenta 1998; Howard 2006; Skocpol 1992), European perspectives on social policy are relevant for the study of American social policy (e.g., Esping-Andersen 1990, 1999), mainly because scholars frequently compare European countries with the United States. Although we should avoid being Eurocentric, we can draw on theories from other countries to shed light on the American welfare state.

Descriptions of social policy often emphasize its relationship to citizenship and the quest for a more inclusive society. For example, according to British sociologist T. H. Marshall (1964), the historical development of modern citizenship is largely about the tension between class inequality stemming from capitalism and the egalitarian logic of citizenship.[2] Marshall's vision of citizenship centers on the multiplication of individual rights related to state expansion. More specifically, the emergence of modern citizenship involves three categories of rights that appear one after the other: civil, political, and social. For Marshall (1964), civil citizenship "is composed of the rights necessary for individual freedom – liberty of the person, freedom of speech, thought and faith, the right to own property and to conclude valid contracts, and the right to justice" (p. 71). But the protection of individual rights like private property favors the emergence of capitalism, which is a direct source of class inequality. According to Marshall, the recognition and extension of political rights, such as the right to vote, exacerbate a tension between capitalist inequality and the egalitarian logic at the core of modern citizenship. For him, recognizing social rights is a way for the state to reduce that tension. Here, social citizenship – and by extension social policy – is largely about income redistribution and state-granted protection against poverty and economic insecurity. This protection takes the form of social rights granted to all citizens. Marshall's universalistic model of social rights is inspired by the United Kingdom's post-war reforms that created universal social benefits covering the entire population (e.g., Glennerster 2000).

In recent decades, a number of scholars have argued that, because of the United States's general lack of universal social programs, the country has no such thing as social citizenship (Fraser and Gordon 1992; Myles 1997). But it is clear that, even in the United States, scholars can follow Marshall's lead in thinking about social policy in terms of citizenship and, more generally, the quest for basic equality and inclusion. For example, feminist scholars like Suzanne Mettler (1998) have used the concept of citizenship to explore the relationship between gender and welfare state development in the United States. Additionally, in the United States and beyond, the concept of citizenship points to philosophical debates about redistributive justice and the idea that all citizens, including the least privileged ones, should have access to a basic "social minimum" as a matter of right (Rawls 1971; see also Smith Barusch 2008: 14–16).

A concept often related to citizenship ever present in the international social policy literature is the idea of solidarity, which is associated with the sociological tradition, notably the work of French sociologist Émile Durkheim (1858–1917). In many Western countries, solidarity has long been a key aspect of the political discourse about the welfare state. This is not an accidental development, because solidarity typically evokes shared, mutual social obligations that can legitimize new and existing social programs. This is why, in a country like France, for example, solidarity and citizenship are closely related political principles central to major social policy debates (Béland and Hansen 2000; Rosanvallon 2000).

In the United States today, the term "solidarity" is seldom featured in mainstream political debates, but that does not mean that public officials never refer to the shared obligations of belonging associated with the concept. For example, in a major 2009 speech to Congress on health-care reform, President Obama referred to broad feelings of national solidarity that, in his mind, justified the extension of health coverage to the population as a whole:

> That large-heartedness – that concern and regard for the plight of others – is not a partisan feeling. It's not a Republican or a Democratic feeling. It, too, is part of the American character – our ability to stand in other people's shoes; a recognition that we are all in this together,

13

and when fortune turns against one of us, others are there to lend a helping hand . . . .

The claim that "we are all in this together" is a powerful expression of solidarity, which is as much a feeling as a rational worldview. Although in everyday life, national solidarity is problematic because of enduring inequalities and group boundaries, the idea that "we are all in this together" can help legitimize the welfare state as well as reform proposals aimed at expanding it.

Related to solidarity but deprived of its emotional component, risk pooling is another prominent aspect of modern social policy (Hacker 2006). For example, risk pooling is a key element of contemporary health-care debates, where the solidaristic claim that "we are all in this together" can take an actuarial meaning. "Pooling ensures that the risk related to financing health interventions is borne by all the members of the pool, not by each contributor individually. Its main purpose is to share the financial risk associated with health interventions for which the need is uncertain" (Smith and Witter 2004: 1). Thus, pooling can be understood as a form of actuarial solidarity through which individuals share financial risks and, as a consequence, increase their level of economic security. At least during periods of prosperity, people do not always perceive the seriousness of the economic risks, such as unemployment or medical debts that they may face, making it harder to justify social programs aimed at pooling these risks (Hacker 2006).

Another distinct way to understand the role of social policy is the concept of de-commodification put forward by Gøsta Esping-Andersen (1990), a Danish sociologist. Starting from Karl Marx's assumption that capitalism is largely about the commodification of labor (i.e., its transformation into a market product), he argues that a central goal of the welfare state is to reduce this dependency of workers and their families on labor-market participation. For him, de-commodification occurs when the state grants workers social rights that are autonomous from their labor-market status: "De-commodification occurs when a service is rendered as a matter of right, and when a person can maintain a livelihood without reliance on the market" (pp. 71–2), while de-commodification stemming from particular social programs "strengthens the worker and weakens the absolute authority of the employer" (p. 72). However, only comprehensive and widely accessible social transfers and services can "substantially emancipate individuals from market dependence" (p. 72). De-commodification does not mean that people should not work; rather, their economic security should be guaranteed autonomously from market outcomes.

In his work, Esping-Andersen stresses that social policy analysis should go beyond general social-spending figures to explore how different types of social programs can result in different levels of de-commodification. For example, low levels of social assistance benefits that are a major source of stigma constitute a "safety net of last resort" (p. 72) and are not a genuine source of de-commodification since these benefits are meant to encourage workers to remain dependent on market outcomes for their survival. Because these benefits do not provide a clear state-granted right to welfare, they exacerbate market dependency instead of emancipating workers and their families from market outcomes. Inspired by both the Marxist tradition and the Scandinavian experience, this model is grounded in the belief that only a strong role by the state can free workers from market dependency and insecurity.

Although it is common to follow Esping-Andersen in defining social policy as a state-led emancipation from market dependency, French sociologist Robert Castel (2003) formulated a slightly different view of the relationship between capitalism and social policy. From his perspective, modern social policy is about transforming the status of workers through the creation of a "wage society" in which employment, traditionally seen as a deprived condition, can become a genuine source of security for workers. Unlike Marshall and Esping-Andersen, who especially value universal services and benefits, Castel argues that modern labor law and social insurance schemes have transformed the social and economic status of wage workers and their families. Instead of following Marshall and Esping-Andersen in thinking about modern social policy as something that emerges in opposition to the market, Castel sees it as an attempt to domesticate the market from within, through the creation of a "wage society" centered on protected employment status. This vision of a wage society is probably rooted in France's social insurance system, which traditionally grants comparatively high levels of social benefits directly related to work experience.[3] What is particularly interesting about Castel's model is that it draws our attention to the central role of labor law and social insurance in modern social policy. The focus on social insurance is crucial in terms of the United States because, as discussed next, its two largest federal social programs are social insurance programs: Medicare and Social Security (Marmor and Mashaw 2006).

From an American perspective at least, the idea that welfare state programs can emerge in close relationship to market forces, rather than in opposition to them, is extremely relevant. In recent decades, a growing number of American scholars have stressed the role of employer-sponsored private benefits in the development of modern social policy. Because private health and pension benefits constitute a legitimate and widespread form of social policy in the United States and, to a lesser extent, Canada, a purely statist approach to social policy focusing exclusively on citizenship and de-commodification is not appropriate in the North American context – although the recent decline in employment-based social benefits, which has been particularly dramatic in the United States since the 1980s, cannot be ignored.

As Jacob Hacker (2002), Christopher Howard (1997), Jennifer Klein (2003), and Jill Quadagno (1988) suggest, scholars must pay close attention to private benefits, and their relationship to public social programs, when studying social policy. Excluding private benefits from the realm of social policy would make it especially difficult to understand the very nature of the "divided" and sometimes "hidden" American welfare state (Hacker 2002; Howard 1997), which is grounded in the complex interactions between public and private schemes discussed in Chapter 2.

This discussion points to the multifaceted nature of social policy, which resists narrow definitions largely due to the different types of social programs that pursue distinct objectives, ranging from poverty alleviation and de-commodification to risk pooling and citizenship inclusion. Under some circumstances, a specific welfare state program can have a number of different goals. For example, Social Security can both fight poverty and help maintain the income of middle-class retirees (Achenbaum 1986; Myles 1988). In fact, from a historical standpoint, social programs can take on new meanings over time, as policymakers alter their core objectives in response to changing economic, political, and social circumstances. In the mid-1960s, for instance, American federal social assistance programs took on a new meaning in the context of the civil rights movement and the quest for racial equality. As Margaret Weir (1992) puts it, "as riots began to shake northern cities, President Johnson looked to the poverty program as a way to funnel resources into the affected black communities" (cited in Thelen 2003: 229). Because the objectives of social programs can change over time, a broad understanding of social policy is vital.

Clearly, social programs can play a number of distinct roles in society, but, at the same time, they are related to other types of public policies. Some social programs have an explicit economic mission, which is analytically distinct from their social policy goals. For example, since the 1960s, the Canadian province of Quebec has invested surpluses from public old-age insurance funds to stimulate provincial economic development (Béland and Lecours 2008). In the post-World War II era,[4] when the ideas of British economist John Maynard Keynes exerted a strong influence on policymakers, European and North American welfare states played an explicit and central role in economic regulation (e.g., stimulating consumer activity during economic downturns) that has been preserved at least in part to this day. Today, social policy domains such as health-care create millions of jobs, which, in turn, has a direct impact on economic development, and even in countries like the United Kingdom and Canada with a strong public health-care system, the private pharmaceutical industry is a major economic player (Walley, Haycox, and Boland 2004). Beyond its relationship to economic development, the welfare state is directly related to education, which is a form of social policy in the broad sense of the term: training programs involve education policy, as does child-care, which is largely about education and the promotion of gender equality and increased female labor-force participation.

Overall, like the welfare state, education policy is central to debates on citizenship and equality in contemporary societies (Olssen, Codd, and O'Neill 2004). However, in terms of formal schooling, it is relevant to distinguish education policy from the welfare state: education is a distinct field of study and a policy area that often requires a particular set of analytical tools (Sykes, Schneider, and Plank 2009). Because education is typically not seen as a component of the welfare state, which is the focus of this book, we do not concentrate on it here. This does not mean, however, that the study of the welfare state should exclude education, which is a key aspect of social policy broadly defined. Thus, even a discussion centered on the welfare state should take education into account.

As well as being related to policy areas such as education and economic policy, the welfare state is sometimes described as part of a broader state mission. In his 2002 book, historian David Moss describes social insurance programs like Medicare and Social Security as examples of state-organized risk management aimed at reducing uncertainty in economic and social life. According to Moss, risk management policy refers to "any governmental activity designed either to reduce or to reallocate risks" (p. 1) and ranges from bankruptcy protection and disaster relief to product liability and social insurance. Thus, following the logic of risk pooling described above, social programs can become risk-management tools in the broader context of the state's role as a last-resort insurer that compensates for "market failures" while contributing to economic regulation and security. Another way to understand social policy as part of an even bigger picture is to depict social programs as examples of "state protection," defined as the general attempt on the part of government to reduce uncertainty and fight global threats, ranging from economic insecurity to environmental disasters and violent attacks.[5] Here, social policy is only one element of the bigger state intervention picture, as this policy area complements other forms of state protection such as environmental policy and national defense. Social policy is a distinct policy area, but we should be aware of its existence in relationship to other policy areas – and even to larger economic, political, and social forces that cannot be understood without looking beyond existing distinctions between narrowly defined policy domains.

Recognizing overlaps between policy areas should not prevent us from emphasizing what is distinct about the *social* programs at the center of the modern welfare state. This is why, throughout this book, social policy refers primarily to programs that aim to support the poor, fight inequality and promote citizenship solidarity, reduce market dependency (i.e., de-commodification), and/ or protect workers and their families against specific economic risks. Certainly, it would be more elegant to define social policy in relationship to just one of these goals; however, it is better to remain open to what social programs *can* do instead of adopting a narrow definition inspired by our normative preferences (what we think these programs *should* do). As for the welfare state, this term generally refers to the aggregation of social programs that have developed in a specific country. Normative definitions of the welfare state that focus on the appropriate level of economic protection that a state should offer are interesting, but they are not used in this book. The concept of welfare state can mean different things to different people, and adopting a clear definition is important to avoid major analytical confusions (Veit-Wilson 2000; Wincott 2003).

Types of Programs

Social programs at the heart of the modern welfare state can be classified in a number of ways. For example, the social policy literature commonly distinguishes between public and private benefits, although, as discussed more extensively in Chapter 2, the public–private mix is rarely straightforward because public policies such as tax incentives and regulations impact the development of private benefits (Béland and Gran 2008; Hacker 2002; Howard

1997). Another important distinction is between income maintenance and social services, which is not about distributing money
to people but about providing them with services, ranging from
health-care to training opportunities. This distinction between
cash benefits and services is present across social policy areas. For
example, unemployment policies can provide insurance benefits
to people who have lost their job but they can also offer them
the opportunity to improve their occupational skills through
subsidized internships and training courses. Often, the provision of health and services requires more staff and a greater
involvement of professionals than the allocation of cash benefits,
especially when it takes the form of tax credits, which are generally administered by existing tax agencies.

To this basic distinction between income maintenance and
social services, we can add a typology that draws a line between
programs according to their eligibility criteria and financing
mechanisms. For the sake of clarity, our discussion focuses on
three main, and sometimes overlapping, well-known program
types: social assistance, social insurance, and universal transfers
and services (e.g., O'Connor 2002; Olsen 2002: 27–31; Rice and
Prince 2000; see Table 1.1).

Table 1.1 Three types of social program

Type	Financing	Benefits	Example
Social assistance	General revenues	Income and/or means-tested	Temporary Aid for Needy Families (TANF)
Social insurance	Payroll tax (but can be supplemented by general revenues)	Benefits tied to past payroll contributions	US Social Security
Universal transfers and services	General revenues is most common	Benefits available to all residents as a right	British National Health Service (NHS)

Social Assistance

The oldest type of social program within this typology is social assistance, which only targets poorer citizens. There are two main ways for the state to determine who is eligible to receive social assistance transfers and services: means-testing and income-testing, which are sometimes combined.

Means-tested programs are only accessible to unemployed or low-income people whose assets fall under a specific threshold. For example, in some jurisdictions, people who own their house or have significant personal savings are not eligible for social assistance benefits; only people considered truly needy (those without major assets to support themselves) would qualify. Residency criteria can supplement the means test, which may exclude poor immigrants from receiving social assistance benefits. In the United States, a well-known example of means-tested program is the Temporary Aid to Needy Families (TANF).

Pure income-tested programs do not consider assets when determining eligibility. The principal eligibility condition is low income, sometimes supplemented by residency criteria. Canada's Guaranteed Income Supplement (GIS) is a good example of a large-scale income-tested program in North America. In terms of retirement security, the GIS provides a much larger benefit than the American Supplemented Security Income (SSI), at least on a per capita basis (the Canadian population is almost ten times smaller than the American population). The liberal eligibility criteria of the GIS makes it a much more efficient tool for fighting poverty among the elderly than its American counterpart (SSI), which is both means-tested and income-tested. However, the fact that GIS benefits are more generous and accessible to elderly people also means they create a greater fiscal burden for all taxpayers (Wiseman and Yčas 2008). This is true because social assistance programs like the GIS and SSI are typically financed through the state's general revenues. Social assistance programs are explicitly redistributive, in the sense that wealthier taxpayers who may never qualify for benefits contribute to cash payments and services allocated to people who, in some circumstances, are too poor to pay income taxes.

21

This overt redistribution is a major aspect of the politics of social assistance, in that citizens may object to paying taxes that finance benefits allocated to less well-off people who, in their opinion, do not deserve state support. This aspect points to the traditional distinction between "deserving" and "undeserving" poor, which can be traced back to the debate on the British Poor Law (Castel 2003; Polanyi 2001) and is rooted in the assumption that only some poor people truly deserve social assistance benefits. What makes the poor deserving varies depending on the historical and social context but can include factors such as disability and age (too old or too young). The undeserving poor are seen as lazy, morally inferior individuals who have a tendency to exploit the excessive generosity of taxpayers instead of looking for a job and fending for themselves (Steensland 2007). Frequently tainted by class, gender, ethnic, or racial stereotypes, this type of discourse was constant in the American welfare debate that raged from the late 1960s to 1996, when President Bill Clinton signed legislation ending the controversial Aid to Families with Dependent Children (AFDC) program. In the United States, the term "welfare," as used in the AFDC program and in the Temporary Aid to Needy Families (TANF) program, which replaced it, has become synonymous with social assistance.

But as Christopher Howard (2006) convincingly argues, it would be a mistake to generalize from that welfare debate to depict all programs for the poor as politically vulnerable. Such a generalization (e.g., Skocpol 1990) would imply that political support for social assistance policies is necessarily much lower than support for social insurance schemes like Medicare and Social Security. Instead, as Howard illustrates, a number of major American social assistance programs are both popular and politically sustainable. For example, since the late 1980s, coverage for Medicaid has expanded (Brown and Sparer 2003) without creating a political backlash. Other social assistance programs, such as the Earned Income Tax Credit (EITC) program and the Children's Health Insurance Program (CHIP) are also popular, and their expansion is often seen as legitimate. Both programs target populations that are seen as deserving of state assistance – the working poor (EITC) and low-income children (CHIP) – and contradict the common wisdom that social assistance programs are necessarily vulnerable from a political standpoint (Howard 2006). To assess the social and political status of an assistance program, it is essential to account for factors such as the perception of its beneficiaries and its relationship to widely shared and historically constructed "categories of worth," such as the dichotomy between the deserving and undeserving poor (Steensland 2007; for a similar perspective see Fraser and Gordon 1994).

Social Insurance

Access to social assistance is need- or income-based, but entitlement to social insurance benefits typically stems from payroll contributions. Under most social insurance arrangements, in order to qualify for benefits, people must have contributed (through the payroll tax) for a minimum time period, which varies from one program to another. In the United States, Social Security is structured in this way. As for unemployment insurance, in the vast majority of American states, only employers pay social insurance contributions. This is a major distinction from Social Security, to which both workers and employers contribute equally.

Most income programs that operate according to social insurance principles are meant to maintain people's standard of living after retirement or during periods of disability or unemployment, and a relationship exists between the wage people earn and the level of cash benefits they receive once they qualify for benefits. In the case of old-age insurance programs such as Social Security, full benefits are only available after a certain age (sixty-six years old as of 2009), while for health insurance schemes, coverage stems from payroll contributions. Sometimes, the term "health insurance" is used misleadingly to refer to universal schemes in which entitlement is tied not to contributions but rather to citizenship or residency. For instance, because health-care entitlement in Canada is based on citizenship and residency, its provincially operated public health-care system is not grounded in strict social insurance principles.[6] The status of the Medicare program in the

United States is different, as some of its key components operate according to social insurance principles, including – payroll – contribution financing (Marmor and Mashaw 2006).

In the field of old-age security, the relationship between contributions and benefits is at the heart of the social insurance logic. This relationship has led to a political discourse according to which workers' payroll contributions create "earned rights," which in turn create entitlements that simply allow retirees to "get back" the money they had previously "put in" during their working years. This discourse is especially prevalent in the United States, where supporters of Social Security have long depicted the program as a source of earned rights, similar to a savings scheme. From a political standpoint, this view has helped shield the program from conservative attacks by depicting it as an institution that is consistent with so-called "American values" like self-reliance and personal responsibility (Béland 2005). Although the metaphor of earned rights is relevant, it is potentially misleading. Social Security is a pay-as-you-go system that essentially transfers money from workers to current retirees, so people who receive Social Security benefits do not actually get "their" money back. Instead, they receive money from active workers who currently pay Social Security contributions. Furthermore, people who live a longer-than-average life sometimes receive far more in Social Security benefits than they ever contributed to the program. In fact, during the post-World War II era, the first cohorts of Social Security beneficiaries received more money than they ever paid in. At the time, favorable demographic conditions related to the Baby Boom (i.e., many younger workers would soon enter the job market and pay contributions) helped make this situation possible (Schieber and Shoven 1999).

Regarding social insurance schemes, if people can get more than what they paid in, the opposite is also true. For instance, people with very stable jobs can pay unemployment insurance contributions during their whole career without ever receiving unemployment benefits, and people who die at age sixty, after having contributed to Social Security for three or four decades, never receive a dime from the program (although their survivors could receive benefits derived from their contributions).

In the end, social insurance is about risk pooling, and some people do get a better deal than others. Still, this does not necessarily weaken the legitimacy of social insurance because it is hard for individuals to predict, decades in advance, how they will fare in terms of their health, employment status, and life expectancy. Unlike personal savings schemes, social insurance programs set benefit levels in advance so people have a better idea of what they should receive in the future. But as with all public policies, social insurance programs are historical constructions that can be transformed, over time, by political decisions. In other words, social insurance is a form of risk management and a genuine source of economic security that is not immune from cutbacks and other political attacks. As authors such as Paul Pierson (1994) have argued, although the relationship between contributions and benefits and the existence of large armies of beneficiaries entitled to benefits can protect these programs from direct political threats, cutbacks and restructurings always remain possible. From a political perspective, citizens should never take social programs for granted – they may have to fight to expand or even to preserve them.

Universal Transfers and Services

In some countries, a number of social programs are universal, in the sense that all citizens and even permanent residents are automatically entitled to certain income transfers and social services as a matter of right. The term "universal" is paradoxical, however, because *national* social programs, including universal transfers and services, typically exclude outsiders – people who do not live in or do not belong to the particular country – from receiving benefits. Thus, many social programs are about political membership and/or residency status, which is partly why, as evidenced in Chapter 5, immigration and social policy intersect.

Universal transfers and services differ from social insurance systems in that they are exclusively or largely financed through general revenues. There are two main types of universal transfers and services: demogrants and universal provisions. Demogrants are policies that are available to people of a certain age who meet specific citizenship and residency criteria. For example, from 1944 to the 1980s, Canadian parents received family allowances for each of their children, from birth to adulthood. Another Canadian demogrant is Old Age Security (OAS), a modest, flat old-age pension, which was adopted in 1951 and is formally available to all people aged sixty-five and older who meet certain residency criteria. In contrast, universal provisions are available to all people, regardless of age, as long as they meet similar citizenship and residency criteria (Béland and Myles 2005). In Canada, public health-care is universal, which means that any citizen or permanent resident is entitled to a wide range of health services anywhere in the country, despite the fact that each of the ten provinces – and not the federal government – operates the public system (Rice and Prince 2000).

Unlike Canada but also the United Kingdom and Sweden, the United States has not developed universal public social programs that cover its entire population and that are based solely on citizenship and/or residency criteria. Although some components of Medicare are similar to the demogrant logic, the American welfare state centers, for the most part, on the dichotomy between social assistance and social insurance (Fraser and Gordon, 1992). This is partly a historical legacy of the New Deal, whereby President Franklin Roosevelt and others promoted the expansion of Social Security by criticizing social assistance and rejecting proposals for the creation of universal benefits like a flat federal pension (Cates 1983). During the late 1960s and 1970s, an attempt to create a guaranteed income system to replace existing American welfare programs failed because it involved covering different categories of people under what many observers wrongly understood as a new form of "welfare" (Steensland 2007).[7]

Today, there is no truly universal public social program in the United States. Overall, the relative absence of universal transfers and services in the United States points to the lack or, at least, the weakness of social citizenship in the country (Fraser and Gordon 1992). Yet, in that country, the gradual expansion of health insurance coverage central to the 2010 health-care reform

(Chapter 5) may facilitate the advent of a universalistic model of social rights.

A type of social benefit directly related to citizenship, but not a demogrant in the strict sense of the term, are programs to assist current and former military personnel and their families. From pensions to health-care to educational provisions, social policies for the military are a major aspect of the modern welfare state. For example, in the United States, as in many other countries, military pensions emerged long before the advent of comprehensive public pensions for the general population: a striking example is the expansion of Civil War pensions in late nineteenth- and early twentieth-century America (Skocpol 1992). But pensions are only one aspect of the safety net offered to veterans. For instance, the GI Bill (Servicemen's Readjustment Act), which was enacted in 1944, provided returning American veterans with unemployment benefits, low-interest home loans, tuition assistance, and vocational training, among other things. Accessible to all veterans regardless of racial and ethnic background, the GI Bill became a source of citizenship inclusion and social mobility during the post-war era (Mettler 2005). Recently, access to quality health-care for US veterans has become a major political issue. In 2006, for example, veterans' groups accused the Bush administration of potentially depriving thousands of veterans of health coverage through insufficient funding (United States House of Representatives 2006).

Beyond veterans, it is important to keep in mind that, in the United States like in most other countries, the army provides health, housing, and social benefits to military personnel in active service. Frequently excluded from mainstream social policy analysis, this "camouflaged safety net" has recently been depicted as a low-profile yet highly significant component of the American welfare state (Gifford 2006). Overall, given that military service is a key form of citizenship participation and is related to highly symbolic and emotional issues, like patriotism and self-sacrifice, the fate of the safety net for soldiers and veterans is a potentially controversial issue, in the United States and beyond.

Policy Areas

The previous discussion referred to concrete social programs located within specific policy areas, but it is now time to systematically highlight broad differences between these areas. In effect, social programs deal with distinct social and economic problems that shape their structure and character beyond the distinctions between social assistance, social insurance, and universal transfers and services. To give you a good idea of the substantial diversity on the field of social policy, this section compares and contrasts five policy areas at the center of the modern welfare state: (1) work, unemployment, and welfare; (2) pensions; (3) health-care; (4) housing; and (5) family benefits (see Table 1.2). Throughout

Table 1.2 Five social policy areas

Policy area	Possible objectives	Public programs	Private benefits
Work, unemployment, and welfare	Providing cash support and services to jobless people or low-income workers	Unemployment insurance; Earned Income Tax Credit (EITC)	Severance packages offered by employers
Pensions	Providing income support for the disabled, elderly people, and survivors	Social Security; Supplemental Security Income (SSI)	Private pensions and personal savings accounts
Health care	Favoring access to health services and help pay medical bills	Medicare; Medicaid; Children's Health Insurance Program (CHIP)	Employer-sponsored and personal health insurance coverage
Housing	Help people afford a home; preventing homelessness	Public housing facilities; vouchers; mortgage deduction	Employer-sponsored housing and relocation packages
Family benefits	Child welfare; gender equality; education; work–family balance	Publicly funded child-care; parental leave entitlements	Private child-care and employer-sponsored (paid) parental leaves

this discussion, it is crucial to acknowledge the relationship between public and private social programs as well as the role of regulations and tax schemes that shape these private programs. As suggested above, taking public–private interactions into account is especially crucial when we study the United States, a country where these interactions have largely shaped welfare state development (e.g., Hacker 2002; Howard 2006; Klein 2003).

Work, Unemployment, and Welfare

Being out of work or earning low wages is a primary source of poverty and economic insecurity in capitalist societies, and it is why governments enact social insurance and social assistance programs for the unemployed and the poor. Programs can provide cash benefits, job training and educational opportunities, or in-kind provisions such as Food Stamps, a federal social assistance scheme that helps eligible poor people buy food using a special debit card (the actual stamps are long gone).

From a historical standpoint, unemployment is a relatively new policy concept, which crystallized in the late nineteenth and early twentieth century (Topalov 2000; Walters 2000). Unemployment is not only about being jobless – it is about being jobless while actively looking for work. Thus, in general, jobless people who are not seeking employment are not officially considered unemployed. Because official unemployment rates exclude jobless people not currently looking for work, these rates are potentially decep-tive. For instance, people who think they cannot find a job due to an economic crisis and decide to stop looking for one will not be added to the list of unemployed people. Moreover, severance packages offered by employers are more likely to make a differ-ence for well-paid employees, including CEOs, who are known for their expensive "golden parachutes."

As a welfare state program, unemployment insurance pro-vides temporary support to the unemployed while they look for work. It is at least partly financed through contributions paid by workers and/or employers, depending on the nature of the scheme. Generally, workers need to be employed for a certain time period before they are eligible to receive benefits. In the United States, the states run unemployment insurance programs and, as a consequence, benefit levels and eligibility criteria vary from state to state. Most other developed countries have adopted more centralized schemes that are operated at the national level. Interestingly, Canada created a federal unemployment insurance system during World War II (Campeau 2005), and since the late 1970s, the system's eligibility criteria have varied from one region to another, depending on unemployment levels (i.e., people living in regions where unemployment is higher can access federal benefits earlier than those living in other regions).

In most developed countries, including the United States, access to unemployment insurance is restricted, and many unemployed individuals do not qualify for benefits. Moreover, people who are entitled to benefits typically receive them for a limited period of time, depending on their work history and the program's eligibility criteria, and some unemployed people end up on social assistance rolls after they run out of insurance benefits. As a result, during economic downturns, social assistance caseloads are likely to increase alongside unemployment insurance rolls, a situation that raises the fiscal burden stemming from both types of programs.

In the United States, access to social assistance programs is limited to some categories of people, generally through a means test and/or an income test, as discussed above. In the post-war era, the most debated social assistance program in the United States was by far the Aid to Families with Dependent Children (AFDC). Created as part of the 1935 Social Security Act, this program, which aimed at providing funding to state programs that supported single mothers living in poverty, became increasingly controversial in the 1960s, when factors like changing family patterns and the struggle against discriminatory (e.g., racist) entitlement rules favored an increase in AFDC rolls (Weaver 2000: 56). "AFDC rolls expanded from 3 million persons (caretakers and children) in 1960 to 4.3 million in 1965 and to 10.2 million in 1971, while combined federal and state expenditures rose from barely $1 billion to $6.2 billion" (Weaver 2000: 55). After three decades of heated welfare debates centered on "work ethics," "family values," and, implicitly, gender and race relations, AFDC was replaced by TANF (Temporary Aid to Needy Families). One consequence of that 1996 federal welfare reform (Personal Responsibility and Work Opportunity Reconciliation Act) is that most TANF beneficiaries are now subject to strict time limits (Waddan 2003; Weaver 2000). For instance, most people cannot stay on welfare for more than two years in a row, and people cannot spend more than five years in total on welfare. States must comply with these time limits to receive full federal welfare funding, which takes the form of a block grant – a fixed sum of money allocated every year, which has replaced traditional federal matching funds. And, compared to unemployment insurance, receiving welfare is a potentially greater source of stigma, partly because benefits are not related to previous contributions, although, as stated earlier, the level of stigma varies from program to program and depends on changing economic, historical, and political circumstances. During periods of economic hardship, for example, the public may hold a more sympathetic view of welfare recipients because they think it is harder to find a job. Overall, together with traditional concerns about work ethics and personal responsibility, changing circumstances impact the politics of unemployment insurance and welfare reform.

In addition to these traditional social assistance programs, the modern welfare state can subsidize low-income workers through a number of schemes, including tax credits like the EITC (Earned Income Tax Credit). Enacted in 1975 as a relatively modest scheme, the EITC is a low-profile social program that has significantly expanded since its creation. As opposed to welfare (e.g., AFDC), the EITC is hardly a controversial program, and its main rationale is to help the working poor through the federal tax system.

> Almost all recipients claim the EITC when filling their annual tax return. The credit reduces the amount of income tax owned and in most cases produces a tax refund. The value of the credit depends on the amount of earned income. . . . In 2003, the EITC reduced the income tax of the eligible family to zero and generated a refund check of $1,600. (Howard 2006: 98)

When exploring the welfare state, especially the American one, taking tax credits like the EITC into account is crucial (Myles and Pierson 1997).

Pensions

Although retirement had existed among privileged occupational groups for some time, it was only during the twentieth century that it gradually became a widespread social institution that shapes the life course of most individuals. The development of modern public pension systems covering all workers proved instrumental in this democratization of retirement (Graebner 1980). Today, a number of developed countries still have mandatory retirement policies, which force many people to retire when they reach a certain age (typically, sixty-five). In the United States, Congress banned mandatory retirement in 1986 as part of a broader push to fight age-based discrimination (Ebbinghaus 2006: 210); however, the demise of mandatory retirement has not triggered a decline in retirement as a major institution in American society. As the average life expectancy increases, people tend to rely on retirement pensions for longer than ever before. Partly as a result, pension expenditures have gradually increased over the past decades, a trend that should accelerate in the years to come as Baby Boomers (people born between 1946 and 1964) begin to retire. Annual Social Security expenditures ($585 billion in 2007) are already significantly higher than the US defense budget (Sherman 2008). As discussed in Chapter 5, this increasing fiscal burden is central to the contemporary debate on the future of modern public pension systems.

Public systems rely on different types of pension policy. In developed countries, social insurance pensions financed through employer and/or worker contributions are a prominent type of pension policy. The first modern old-age insurance system emerged in Germany in the late nineteenth century; later, countries like Belgium and France followed this social insurance path by enacting occupationally distinct schemes managed by employers and labor organizations. Thus, instead of having one social insurance program for the working population as a whole, these countries created separate schemes covering distinct occupational categories like farmers and industrial workers (Baldwin 1990). The United States adopted a more centralized and statist version of the old-age insurance model first developed in Germany. Known as Social Security, this federal old-age insurance program is complemented by social assistance benefits – in the form of Supplemental Security Income (SSI) – for the elderly poor. But social insurance is not the dominant public pension model in all developed countries. In fact, countries like Australia and New Zealand do not operate a comprehensive public old-age insurance program, which does not mean that the state is not a central player in their respective pension system (Ashton and St John 2008).

Pension programs are long-term commitments that are affected by slow-moving demographic transformations. In the United States, actuarial forecasts for Social Security extend over a seventy-five-year period, which is quite long by most public-policy standards. In effect, the politics of pension reform is largely guided by anxieties about the future, as well as by long-term economic and political imperatives. Although elected officials may tend to focus on short-term problems because of obvious electoral constraints (e.g., members of the US House of Representatives face re-election every two years), recent international studies have concluded that, under particular institutional and ideological conditions, elected officials will take political risks to address perceived long-term problems like a projected imbalance in public pension financing scheduled to occur decades ahead (Jacobs 2008; Little 2008).

In many countries, tax-subsidized private pensions play a major role alongside public retirement benefits like Social Security. For instance, in the United Kingdom, Canada, and the United States, voluntary, loosely regulated and tax-subsidized private pension schemes developed alongside the public pension system (Béland and Gran 2008; Shalev 1996), and this complex articulation of public and private pension programs has led a number of journalists, policymakers, politicians, and pension experts to view them as equal, complementary elements (Leimgruber 2008: 186). For instance, the American pension system has been described as a "three-pillar" model, where Social Security, private pensions, and personal savings complement one another. However, this idea of three pillars, or the related metaphor of the three-legged stool (DeWitt 1996), is misleading because Social Security is not simply one pillar among others but the true foundation of a pension system in which private pensions only cover part of the workforce and personal savings remain limited at best, especially when low-income workers are concerned (apRoberts 2000). Despite this remark, private pension and savings schemes do play a key role in American retirement security, and the federal government has long subsidized these private schemes through massive yet low-profile tax expenditures that disproportionately benefit wealthier people (Hacker 2004; Howard 2006).

In the United States, disability policy is closely related to retirement policy as both Social Security and SSI feature major disability components. Created in 1956 and gradually expanded thereafter, Disability Insurance (DI) is part of the Social Security system and a key aspect of the federal welfare state (more than nine million beneficiaries as of December 2008, out of a total of some fifty-one million Social Security beneficiaries). The disability component of SSI is much larger than its retirement component: in 2008, nearly 90 percent of the seven million SSI beneficiaries were disabled (Social Security Administration 2008: 2). Attempts have been made to control costs by limiting the number of people who were recognized as disabled and, therefore, entitled to benefits (Berkowitz 1987), but assessing whether people applying for DI or SSI benefits are in fact disabled or determining their level of disability is seen as a major challenge. In the end, the politics of disability is largely about defining who is disabled, which means that disability benefits are directly related to health-care issues (Jaeger and Bowman 2005).

Another example of how different components of the welfare state overlap involves workers' compensation schemes, which, to a certain extent, relate to both health and pension issues. In the United States, these schemes were enacted by state legislatures during the first decades of the twentieth century (Moss 1995). The goal was to compensate injured workers, or relatives of workers who died in their workplace, in exchange for the absence of legal actions on their part against employers. Today as in the past, state workers' compensation programs vary significantly from one jurisdiction to another (Sengupta, Reno, and Burton 2007). These territorial variations in program structure and benefit levels point to the relationship between federalism and social policy analyzed in the next chapter.

Health-Care

Compared to cash benefit programs like Social Security, modern health-care systems are extremely complex (Béland, 2010), which makes it typically harder to assess the possible impact of available policy alternatives (the debate about the "real costs" of the 2010 American health reform illustrates this reality). This complexity of health-care as a policy area reflects the above-mentioned distinction between services and cash benefits. "[T]he issues raised by benefits in kind are genuinely complex, and raise trickier problems of mixed public–private involvement than is the case for most cash benefits" (Barr 1993: 289). This feature of contemporary health-care systems is particularly striking in the United States, where various public and private insurance schemes and state regulations have long interacted to create highly intricate institutions (Hacker 2002). Moreover, in the United States as elsewhere, the role of technological innovation in health-care further increases the complexity of that policy area (McClellan and Kessler 2002).

Like other components of the welfare state, health-care policies vary considerably from one country to another (Street 2008). Take health-care financing, for example. One influential form of financing is the single-payer model, in which the state plays the dominant fiscal role (i.e., it pays for most of the basic health-care costs). The United Kingdom and Canada are examples of single-payer health-care systems. But saying that both the United Kingdom and Canada adopted a single-payer model does not mean that they have developed identical health-care systems. For instance, as opposed to the situation prevailing in the United Kingdom, the Canadian state (in this case, the provinces) does not own hospitals. Furthermore, beyond the single-payer model, complex social insurance schemes like those developed in Belgium, France, and Germany can provide universal (or quasi-universal) coverage without the level of statism present in the United Kingdom. And, in a country like Switzerland, the prominent role of private hospitals and insurance companies has not prevented the advent of universal coverage (Bertozzi and Gilardi 2008). These examples are important for students of American health-care policy because they suggest that universal coverage is possible without the creation of a single-payer public health-care system. This does not mean that the creation of such a system would be a bad idea; rather, other options are available as far as reaching universal coverage is concerned.

In the United States, private insurance coverage remains dominant, as both employers and insurance companies provide coverage to most workers and their families in a fragmented private system that is both subsidized and regulated by the state – increasing its complexity. Moreover, through programs like Medicare and Medicaid, the state also plays a direct role in health-care policy. For the most part, these two programs cover people who are traditionally excluded from private health-care coverage: the elderly, the disabled, and (some of) the poor. Yet, although the United States spends more proportionately on health-care than any other country, it is the only developed nation without universal health insurance coverage (Street 2008). In the late 2000s, for example, more than forty-five million people were uninsured at any given time and, among the uninsured, young adults and ethnic and racial minorities were overrepresented (Bolduan 2009; Starr and Fernandopulle 2005). Thus, like poverty, the lack of health coverage is not a randomly distributed social and economic risk. This issue is further discussed in Chapter 5, where we turn to recent political efforts to increase insurance coverage in the United States, especially the 2010 health-care reform.

Housing

One of the most basic human needs is access to adequate housing, which is why, in developed societies and beyond, homelessness is considered a radical form of insecurity and deprivation (Polakow and Guillean 2001). As well as being typically more exposed to violence and criminal activities (Stateman 2008), many homeless people in northern cities die every winter from the cold, despite the availability of a limited number of emergency shelters. Beyond homelessness, even in developed countries like the United States, many low-income individuals and families struggle every month to pay their rent or their mortgage, or they live in unsanitary homes and apartments. These problems can push poor people to the streets, increasing the homeless population.

Developed countries have responded by creating housing policies to support low-income tenants and by stimulating the construction of affordable housing units, among other things. Over the years, the United Kingdom and France, for example, have developed large public-housing systems (Doling 1997). As for the Netherlands, it has created a massive public housing system where more than a third of the population lives. And, unlike the situation in the United Kingdom during the Thatcher years, in the Netherlands, the public housing sector has not declined in recent decades (Brandsen and Helderman 2006). In contrast, in the United States, public housing has long constituted a rather modest policy area. Authorized by the 1937 National Housing Act, public housing has faced a great deal of opposition from conservative leaders who fear "possible competition with the private housing market and the prospect of relocating poor people, especially blacks, to more affluent neighborhoods" (Pierson 1994: 76). In the years following World War II, public housing policy targeted only the poorest citizens, and, as a result, it became increasingly associated with deprived, minority-dominated, inner-city neighborhoods (Popkin et al. 2000; Vale 2000). Although public housing was significantly expanded in the late 1960s and in the 1970s, little more than 1 percent of the American population lived in housing projects by 1980. Additionally, less than 3 percent of the population received allowances for privately rented housing (Pierson 1994: 76). Efforts were made in the 1990s and into the 2000s to improve the quality of life in many housing projects. Another contemporary trend in housing policy is the development of voucher programs aimed at helping poorer Americans to afford a place to live. For example, the federal Housing Choice Voucher Program provides cash assistance to vulnerable social categories like the disabled, the elderly, and low-income families; the program is administered by local public housing agencies (US Department of Housing and Urban Development 2009). Overall, compared to other developed countries like France and the Netherlands, the contemporary American public-housing system is limited, underfunded, and politically vulnerable. As for employers, they seldom provide direct housing support to their employees, and moving expenses are usually reserved for better-off workers.

There is, however, another aspect of American housing policy that students of the welfare state should consider: home mortgage interest deduction, which allows many homeowners to reduce their income tax burden proportionally to the interests they pay on their mortgage.[8] Adopted in 1913, this low-profile fiscal scheme has gained greater political support over the years. The rapid expansion of individual income taxes during World War II increased the role of home mortgage interest deduction, affecting many more people, including members of the middle class who had to pay federal income tax for the first time ever. After 1945, this policy reinforced the federal push for private middle-class residential construction and, to a certain extent, constituted a hidden, indirect subsidy to the American construction industry (Glaeser and Shapiro 2002: 2). Typically, well-off citizens disproportionately benefit from the deduction, which, in 1995, accounted for an annual revenue loss for the federal government of more than $50 billion (Howard 1997); at the same time, other fiscal schemes that explicitly promote home ownership (e.g., deferring capital gains on the sale of principal residences) cost the federal treasury billions of dollars annually. Because home ownership can become a major source of economic security for individuals and families (Winter 1999), these policies are "social" in nature, despite being fiscally regressive.

Family Benefits

Family benefits constitute a broad policy area that includes provisions designed to increase the well-being and economic security of parents and their children, as well as other objectives, such as helping parents find a better balance between their domestic and their professional lives. Such benefits are closely related to gender relations and how they evolve over time. In the past, family benefits in developed societies largely reflected traditional gender roles according to which mothers stayed at home to raise children and perform domestic tasks (Skocpol 1992). Although it remains influential, this model has long been challenged by feminists as well as social and economic transformations that have led to higher levels of labor-market participation for mothers. Today, when properly designed, family benefits can reduce gender inequalities instead of helping reproduce them, as they often did in the past (O'Connor, Orloff, and Shaver 1999).

As discussed here, the term "family benefits" is somewhat narrower than "family policy," a term that may extend well beyond the welfare state (Bogenschneider 2004). Family benefits include policies such as child-care programs, family allowances, and parental leaves. Interestingly, in the post-war era, the United States never developed a large-scale, national family allowance program, unlike Canada and many European countries (O'Connor, Orloff, and Shaver 1999: 120). In most of these countries, the goal of family allowances was twofold: to provide financial support to parents and to boost or at least maintain fertility rates. From this perspective, family allowances were part of the demographic regulation of these countries (King 1998: 33). The comparatively high fertility rates prevailing in the United States (currently, 2.1 children per woman) may have reduced the apparent need for family allowances. But today, American parents can take advantage of the Child Tax Credit (CTC), which is worth up to $1,000 per child. Like most federal tax expenditures, however, the CTC is a regressive provision that disproportionately benefits better-off parents (Huang and Shaw 2009).

At the broadest level, family benefits are a significant aspect of the American welfare state. In the first decades of the twentieth century, mothers' pensions – designed primarily with the welfare of children in mind – became one of the first components of its modern social policy system. Grounded in traditional gender roles and actively promoted by reformers, women's organizations, and their political allies, these social assistance schemes were adopted by no fewer than forty states between 1911 and 1920. By 1935, all the American states had adopted a mothers' pension program (Skocpol 1992: 446–7). These modest state-level pensions prepared the way for the creation of the Aid for Dependent Children (ADC, later the AFDC) program during the New Deal, while illustrating how family and social assistance benefits have meshed in the United States. Even today, TANF is explicitly defined as "Temporary Assistance for Needy *Families*" and is aimed at supporting poor parents, especially unemployed ones. Consequently, TANF, just like the EITC (Earned Income Tax Credit), can be said to belong to the areas of family benefits and work, unemployment and welfare (O'Connor, Orloff, and Shaver 1999, 120). This example suggests once again that although typologies are useful for mapping the field of social policy, apparently distinct policy areas are somewhat arbitrary constructions that frequently overlap, in one way or another.

Parental leave is another key form of family benefit. Because of the increasing number of women in the job market, parental leave has become a serious social policy issue across the developed world. For many years, the United States lagged behind in that policy area. In fact, before the passage of the 1993 Family and Medical Leave Act (FMLA), it remained one of few developed countries with no national parental leave policy (Haas 2004: 203). Signed by President Bill Clinton, this act grants twelve weeks of unpaid leave to people working for businesses with at least fifty employees (Haas 2004: 203); moreover, "only about 60 percent of all US employees are eligible to take leave under the Family and Medical Leave Act" (Haas 2004: 205). Compared to similar Canadian and European legislation, this act is a modest framework partly because of the unpaid nature of the parental leave enforced by the FMLA. Moreover, as of 2007, only Puerto Rico and five states (California, Hawaii, New Jersey, New York, and Rhode Island) offered paid maternal/parental leaves. Still, employers, even large ones, do not always offer paid leaves to their workers (Lovell, O'Neill, and Olsen,

2007). In general, the United States offers less-comprehensive benefits for parental leave than many other developed countries (O'Connor, Orloff, and Shaver 1999: 4). Finally, it is worth noting that, where parental leaves are concerned, men's take-up rates are typically lower than women's, a situation that reflects at least in part the persistence of traditional gender roles (Kamerman and Gatenio 2002).

Child-care is yet another important form of family benefit in most developed countries. The growing number of women in the formal labor market and the political mobilization of feminist groups have each played a significant role in the expansion of public child-care facilities and programs around the world. Publicly subsidized child-care programs can have several objectives, ranging from economic support for parents to the promotion of gender equality and early childhood education. Since World War II, for example, France and Sweden have created large and widely accessible public systems that explicitly promote gender equality by making it easier for mothers to remain in the labor market. In North America, the French-speaking Canadian province of Quebec has perhaps the most comprehensive public system, with child-care spots in certified facilities available to all parents for just $7 a day (Albanese 2006). The core objectives of this universal scheme are to promote gender equality and to encourage working mothers to have children.

In the United States, comprehensive public child-care for the general population is largely absent, and the state role in child-care policy typically remains limited in scope. But, looking back, we can find some early examples of – limited – state involvement in child-care. For instance, in order to support mothers working in the war industry, "during World War II, the Federal Government sponsored day care for 400,000 preschool children. [Yet] after the war, the Federal Government abdicated all support for day care and instructed women to quit working, go home, and take care of their children" (Boschee and Jacobs 1997). Nonetheless, despite the lack of comprehensive state support since that time, the percentage of working mothers has strongly increased in the United States (as in other developed nations) and, today, most mothers with children aged between three and five work outside the home (Children's Defense Fund 2005: 60).

Not unexpectedly, "as the number of working mothers has increased dramatically over the past three decades, so has the need for reliable, affordable, quality child care" (Children's Defense Fund 2005: 60). In response to these growing child-care demands, the private child-care industry has expanded over the last four decades, and some employers have created facilities to accommodate their employees' children. Indeed, private child-care is a growing industry, which is indirectly subsidized through several provisions of the tax code. Regarding provisions enacted in the late 1970s and early 1980s, Kimberly Morgan (2006) states that such "tax credits helped propel the growth of a private child care market and thus reinforced the public–private divide in the provision of social welfare" (p. 103). Because many employers do not offer or subsidize child-care services, rising costs are a significant concern for working parents, especially poorer ones:

> The average fee for full-time, center-based child care ranges from $3,400 to $14,600 annually, depending on where the family lives and the age of the child. Without child care assistance, low-income families must bear the significant financial burden of paying the full cost of care on their own, and may be unable to afford the high-quality, stable care they want for their children and that parents need [in order] to work. (Schulman and Blank 2008: 1)

Low-income families spend a greater proportion of their income on child-care than their more affluent counterparts and, partly to address this issue, states operate child-care assistance programs for poorer parents, including those who work or study full-time. However, even though these assistance policies clearly increase the economic autonomy and well-being of many low-income parents, "the large majority of states [have] made little progress in these policies, and some states [have] slid backwards. Moreover, in most of these policies, most states had lost ground or failed to move forward since 2001" (Schulman and Blank 2008: 1).

In terms of early childhood education, the federal government plays a significant role through the Head Start program. Created in 1965, this program offers preschool education and social services that are aimed at getting low-income children ready for regular school (Head Start Impact Study 2005: iii). More generally, however, compared to other developed nations, the United States offers relatively limited public support for both child-care and early childhood development (O'Connor, Orloff, and Shaver 1999: 4).

Conclusion

This chapter has highlighted the many-sided nature of social policy, which is divided among types of programs and policy areas. At the same time, the broader meaning of social policy and its direct relationship to issues such as citizenship, poverty, inequality, risk pooling, solidarity, de-commodification, and economic insecurity have been discussed. The relationship between the welfare state and each of these issues varies from program to program, and this is precisely why it is crucial to take into account the diverse social programs that have been created over the years to address such issues. In Chapter 2, we take a more systematic look at key social policy differences that exist between the United States and other developed countries; instead of focusing on types of programs and policy areas, we explore international trends and patterns in order to locate the United States within them. Although Chapter 1 gave you some idea of the policy differences and similarities between the United States and other developed countries, to make sense of this cross-national landscape, we must review the comparative literature on social policy and, more specifically, on welfare regimes.

2

The United States in International Context

Being born in a country other than the United States, you would probably have different expectations about the level of social protection available to you. For example, while Britons and Canadians learn from a young age that equal access to health-care is a right of citizenship, in a country like the United States, this very idea is a major source of controversy. This was clear during the 2009–10 debate on health-care reform, where many conservatives openly rejected the idea that health-care should become a right of citizenship. Although the 2010 reform should considerably reduce the number of uninsured in the United States, the fact that the idea of health-care as a right remains contested in that country is a major difference with most other developed societies, where this idea is now widely shared. In general, despite the impact of the 2010 reform (Chapter 5), the American health-care system remains very different from the single-payer model developed in countries like Canada and the United Kingdom, for example. And this is only one of the many social policy differences between the United States and other developed countries (Chapter 1). Considering this, how do we make sense of such social policy differences between countries?

From a comparative standpoint, social policy is a fragmented landscape, where both transnational and intra-country variations abound. The main objective of this chapter is to map the inter-national social policy landscape and position the United States within it. Through a discussion of the concept of welfare regime, we identify and explain the factors that may distinguish one country's social programs from those of another. To highlight what is specific about the American welfare state in a comparative context, we draw upon the vast international literature on welfare regimes, especially the debate on the work of sociologist Gøsta Esping-Andersen. Despite its limitations, his welfare regime typology remains insightful because it stimulates comparative research and thinking by encouraging us to systematically place our country in its broad international context. For instance, although the United States remains "exceptional" in many respects, it shares a number of trends with other members of the "liberal welfare regime."

This chapter has three main sections. The first section begins by exploring Esping-Andersen's welfare regime typology; it then highlights its possible shortcomings, which leads to a discussion on issues such as gender and race and their relationship to these welfare regimes. If we focus so much on Esping-Andersen's work, it is not because it is the only way to map the international social policy landscape, but because he is one of the most prominent scholars in the field. Even when not agreeing with his typology, many students of social policy engage with his work, and it is useful to know it in order to understand key social science debates about the welfare state. The second section explores the nature of the public–private mix in social policy, which is a key aspect of the liberal welfare regime in which the United States so neatly fits. After exploring differences between countries, welfare regimes, and public–private programs, the third section turns to the territorial logic of social policy within countries, with an emphasis on federalism and the territorial organization of the welfare state, before illustrating how social policy relates to the construction of territorial inequalities and identities.

The Great Welfare Regime Debate

The most common way to take a systematic look at cross-national differences in social policy development is to examine the concept of "welfare regime" as articulated by Gøsta Esping-Andersen

(1990, 1999) and then compare it to the idea of the "welfare state."[1] Traditionally, the welfare state refers explicitly to the role of the state, while the concept of welfare regime has a much broader meaning. For instance, according to Esping-Andersen, a welfare regime is based on a specific relationship between the state, the market, and the family. Inspired by the work of Richard Titmuss (1963a), Esping-Andersen uses his concept of welfare regime to differentiate the ways in which countries organize their social programs in relationship to families and markets. The most important aspect of Esping-Andersen's typology is de-commodification, which, as suggested in Chapter 1, takes place when social transfers and services are granted on the basis of social rights and as a way to make citizens less dependent on the job market for their basic economic security. This focus on de-commodification emphasizes that state-granted social rights should be understood in relationship to market forces. From this perspective, an increase in state-allocated social protection reduces the need for alternative, market-based forms of social policy. The same remark applies to the interaction between the state and the family, as comprehensive public programs are likely to reduce the reliance of individuals on traditional family solidarity. In this domain, the equivalent of de-commodification is labeled "de-familialization." For Esping-Andersen (1990, 1999), public social programs in fields such as employment and family policy can reduce the economic dependence of citizens – and especially women – on their family. In effect, to understand the key differences between how countries allocate welfare, we must not only focus on the public sector but also on the relationship between states, markets, and families.

With its emphasis on the scope and the nature of cross-national differences, Esping-Andersen's typology helps us classify countries into broad categories known as welfare regimes. Each regime is characterized by a unique division of labor between the state, the market, and the family. This division of labor is not just about relative levels of government expenditures (how much money a country allocates to social programs in general); it also considers how each state spends money (what types of benefits and targeted populations are stressed) and how much room is left for family- and market-based social protection. According to Esping-Andersen (1990, 1999), there are three welfare regimes in developed societies – liberal, conservative, and social democratic – and these regimes consist of clusters of countries that, despite their differences, share major similarities. Esping-Andersen has defined them in this way in order to draw our attention to the "big picture," in this case the dominant institutional configurations that characterize each country, rather than the variations that exist between policy areas in just one country. His topology, then, like all typologies, is an explicit simplification of the sheer complexity that characterizes each national social policy system.

In general, the main goal of a typology featuring "families of nations" (Castles 1993) is simply to map a broad research area (in our case, social policy) – not to replace more detailed analyses centered on concrete programs and policy areas. These analyses remain necessary even when doing comparative research, and welfare regimes are simply analytical tools that can help us develop more informed empirical analyses. Moreover, within a particular policy area, two countries belonging to distinct welfare regimes can have more in common than countries within the same regime. For example, in the field of health-care, the United Kingdom, which belongs to the liberal welfare regime, is more similar to social-democratic Sweden than to the United States, another member of the liberal regime.[2] Given these issues, Esping-Andersen (1990) recognizes that "there is no single pure [national] case" and that exogenous elements (i.e., tendencies associated with the two other welfare regimes) exist within each country and each regime (p. 28). Finally, in his seminal 1990 book, he focuses on the crystallization of the three clusters of countries, also called regimes, during the post-World War II era, not on the transformations that have taken place since the mid-1970s (Esping-Andersen 1990). Thus, it is essential to keep all of these points in mind as we briefly review the key differences between the three welfare regimes at the center of this widely debated typology.

Esping-Andersen (1990) describes the liberal welfare regime as a cluster of countries where "means-tested, assistance, modest universal transfers, or modest social insurance plans predominate. Benefits cater mainly to a clientele of low-income, usually working-class, state dependents. Entitlement rules are . . . strict and often associated with stigma; benefits are typically modest. In turn, the state encourages the market, either passively – by guaranteeing only a minimum – or actively – by subsidizing private welfare schemes" (p. 26). He uses "liberal" in the European sense of the term to designate market-friendly beliefs and institutions (in contrast, in the United States, "liberal" is tied to statist, left-leaning thinking). In his typology, countries belonging to this welfare regime include Australia, Canada, the United Kingdom, and the United States. Characterized by lower levels of public benefits and a greater reliance on market-based programs than other countries, members of the liberal cluster are implicitly associated with the Anglo-American "liberal tradition," which authors like Louis Hartz (1955) have traced back to the ideas of British political theorist John Locke (1632–1704).

In the conservative welfare regime, market principles are less dominant than in the liberal regime. Instead, the conservative regime centers on a corporatist tradition that promotes the fragmentation of social policy by increasing the number of social insurance schemes that are aimed at offering separate protection to distinct occupational categories. Effectively, in the context of this regime, the state explicitly promotes the reproduction of occupational inequalities. As for the role of purely private benefits, it remains more limited in scope than in the liberal regime. Finally, compared to the liberal and social-democratic regimes, the conservative cluster is characterized by a stronger emphasis on traditional gender roles and family relations: "Social insurance typically excludes non-working wives, and family benefits encourage motherhood. Day care, and similar family services, are conspicuously underdeveloped" (Esping-Andersen 1990: 27). The preservation of both occupational inequalities and traditional gender roles explains why this regime is "conservative." In the context of Esping-Andersen's typology, social conservatism related to occupational fragmentation and traditional family values is distinct from what is known in the United States as "economic conservatism" (i.e., the pro-market approach tied to the liberal welfare regime). Members of the conservative cluster include Austria, France, Germany, and Italy. As a consequence the focus is not on the Anglo-American world but on continental (Western) Europe, with the notable exception of the Nordic countries belonging to the social-democratic regime.

The social-democratic regime is a cluster of smaller countries – Denmark, Finland, Norway, and Sweden – in which the state plays a bold role by promoting equality, universalism, and de-commodification. Universal services and transfers frequently obviate the need for any strong reliance on private benefits or family support. Thus, the state is by far the dominant actor in social policy, and market providers typically play a much smaller role than in the liberal regime. Moreover, the social-democratic state promotes full employment, rather than maintaining low minimum wages, which is often the case in liberal countries, and socializes the costs of child-care and parenthood through comprehensive, publicly sponsored family benefits. As opposed to the conservative regime, "the idea is not to maximize dependence on the family, but [on] capacities for individual independence. . . . The result is a welfare state that grants transfers directly to children, the aged, and the helpless. It is, accordingly, committed to a heavy social-service burden, not only to service family need but also to allow women to choose work rather than household" (Esping-Andersen 1990: 28). Indeed, social-democratic countries actively promote gender equality through large public programs and universal social services. From a fiscal standpoint, as a direct effect of its reliance on universal, tax-funded social programs, the social-democratic regime is characterized by higher levels of taxation than the liberal regime. Yet, although people living in social-democratic countries pay more income tax than in most other developed societies, citizens in conservative countries tend to face high social insurance contribution rates. As for inhabitants of liberal countries such as Canada, the United Kingdom, and the United States, they pay lower combined (income and payroll) tax rates on average but are likely to spend more on private insurance premiums and other market-related fees (see Tables 2.1 and

49

Table 2.1 Average tax rate on employment income [income and payroll taxes combined] (2004) single individuals without children earning US$37,500 [CDN$40,000] a year

Canada	25
France	28
Germany	38
Italy	30
Japan	17
Sweden	31
UK	24
USA	24

Source: Adapted from Laurin 2006

Table 2.2 Net public and private social expenditures as a percentage of GDP

	Public	Private
Canada	19.6	4.0
France	29.2	2.1
Germany	28.4	3.0
Italy	24.1	1.3
Japan	18.6	3.5
Sweden	28.0	2.6
UK	23.1	4.2
USA	16.9	9.0

Source: Adapted from Organization for Economic Co-operation and Development (Adema and Ladaique 2005: 32)

2.2). In the end, most citizens end up paying for social policy, in one way or another. Although not its primary focus, the welfare regime typology highlights the respective role of different forms of social policy financing.

Partly because there is no consensus in the international social policy literature about how to classify countries, Esping-Andersen's typology of welfare regimes is the starting point of a lively social science debate on cross-national differences and social policy classifications. This international literature has become a growth industry (e.g., Arts and Gelissen 2006; Bonoli 1997;

Castles and Mitchell 1992; Kasza 2002; Lewis 1992; Merrien 1997; O'Connor 2002; Sainsbury 1999) and summarizing it would require publishing a separate book exclusively on this topic. Here, the goal is simply to highlight several key issues raised in this contemporary debate.

First, scholars have argued that some developed countries do not fit neatly into Esping-Andersen's threefold typology. For example, a fourth type of welfare regime could be added to account for the allegedly distinct nature of social policy in East Asian (Jones 1993) or Southern European (Ferrera 1996) countries. The case of Japan is interesting here, as this country features key elements of both the conservative and the liberal welfare regimes, with recent changes pushing it closer and closer to the liberal cluster (Shinkawa 2008). In general, we may need more than three regimes to adequately map dominant social policy patterns within the developed world (Arts and Gelissen 2006). Moreover, attempts have been made to create an alternative typology that offers a more accurate and complex description of cross-national differences and similarities. For instance, Giuliano Bonoli's (1997) welfare regime typology centers on the relationship between spending levels ("how much") and institutional patterns ("how"); by changing the assumptions about the main sources of cross-national differences and similarities, Bonoli ends up with a slightly different typology than Esping-Andersen's.[3]

Second, and more critical to this introduction to social policy, feminist scholars have extensively criticized Esping-Andersen's typology (e.g., Lewis 1992; Mahon 2001; O'Connor, Orloff, and Shaver 1999; Orloff 1993b; Sainsbury 1999). In particular, feminist scholars claim that his typology neglects a dominant aspect of the social world that is crucial for women: the relationship between paid and unpaid work. This neglect gives a different meaning to the issue of de-commodification at the heart of Esping-Andersen's work. From this gendered perspective, "analysis of de-commodification must be accompanied by analysis of services that facilitate labour market participation, such as childcare and parental leave. It is also important to recognize that the unpaid caring work in the home, generally done by women, facilitates the labour force participation of others, generally men" (O'Connor 2002: 122). In effect, the status of women within and outside the family is a key structural aspect of welfare regimes, something that Esping-Andersen (1999) has acknowledged in his more recent work.

One particular focus of the feminist push to create gendered welfare regime typologies is the "male breadwinner model," an ideology present to various degrees across countries (Lewis 1992). In its purest form, this ideology states that women should stay at home to take care of the family through unpaid work, while men should remain the sole breadwinner of the household, working outside the home as part of the paid labor market. Because cross-national variations in this ideology can account for significant differences in program design and gender inequality, these variations are at the center of Jane Lewis's (1992) typology of welfare regimes, which draws a line between "weak," "modified," and "strong" male-breadwinner countries. Lewis's work has been criticized by other feminist scholars, who have developed alternative typologies to capture cross-national variations in the relationship between gender and social policy (O'Connor, Orloff, and Shaver 1999; Sainsbury 1999).

Feminist critiques of Esping-Andersen's work have become a central feature of the contemporary debate on the relationship between gender and social policy, drawing our attention to the gendered nature of social programs, which both reflect and impact patterns of inequality between women and men. While Esping-Andersen focuses mainly on class inequality and decommodification, the recent feminist literature on welfare regimes forces us to adopt a broader vision of inequality when comparing countries and even policy areas within a country. To a certain extent, this feminist literature is not so much a repudiation of Esping-Andersen's typology as an attempt to amend it in favor of a more subtle understanding of the inequality–social policy nexus. As stated in the previous chapter, one of the most significant goals of social programs is to reduce inequality and promote citizenship inclusion. What feminist scholars are telling us is that gender is a critical aspect of this task and that some countries and programs are doing a better job than others at fighting gender inequality and promoting equal citizenship for both women and men (Mettler 1998; O'Connor, Orloff, and Shaver 1999).

A third issue, one that is seldom raised in the existing welfare regime literature, is the impact of race and ethnic relations (Banting and Kymlicka 2007: 22–3).[4] Traditionally, these issues have been less prominent in European than in North American policy debates, which perhaps is why students of race and welfare state development may dismiss the welfare regime literature altogether (Lieberman 2005: 61). One thing is clear, however, at least from an American perspective: those who attempt to gain a comparative understanding of the specific features of the American welfare state should always keep ethnic and race relations in mind. Race, for example, has long been a major factor in American social policy, and even a quick look at American poverty and income-inequality data (Rothenberg 2006) suggests that, despite recent progress, citizenship equality and social inclusion remain works-in-progress. Further, as Robert Lieberman (1998) has argued, depending on their key institutional features, social programs can have different effects on patterns of racial inequality. Thus, any comparative perspective on welfare state development in the United States should stress the central role of racial inequality in American society, an issue that concerns both African Americans whose ancestors came to the United States a long time ago as slaves and other minorities who have recently settled in the country as a result of voluntary immigration. Most immigrant groups are poorer on average than the general population and, as evidenced by the debate surrounding the 1996 welfare reform, their status in relationship to social programs can become a serious political issue. Finally, although Native Americans form only a small percentage of the American population, they face a great deal of economic and social hardship that is directly related to social policy issues. In Australia, Canada, and New Zealand, meanwhile, partly because aboriginal peoples form a larger percentage of the overall population, aboriginal concerns are prominent policy issues (Papillon and Cosentino 2004).

Although ethnic and racial inequality should clearly be at the forefront of many North American social policy debates, it would be a mistake to discard the welfare regime approach simply because it does not focus on these issues. For instance, understanding the nature of the liberal welfare regime can help explain how its greater reliance on private benefits can exacerbate not only class and gender but also racial and ethnic inequalities. Minorities are often disadvantaged in the labor market, a situation that makes them less likely on average to access social benefits through their employer (Howard 2006; Klein, 2003). The issue of access to benefits through an employer leads us now to the discussion of the role of the public–private mix in the American-liberal-welfare regime.

Private Benefits in the Liberal Welfare Regime

Despite the legitimate criticisms formulated against Esping-Andersen's typology, his approach, like that of Titmuss (1963a), highlights the relationship between capitalism (markets), public policy (states), and social inequality. The recent growth in scholarship on the relationship between public and private social policy in the United States can be placed against the comparative backdrop of the welfare regime literature (Béland and Gran 2008). Although the strong reliance of the United States on private social benefits is spectacular (Ghilarducci 2008; Hacker 2002; Howard 1997; Klein 2003; Quadagno 1988), other countries, especially those associated with the liberal welfare regime, feature the development of massive publicly subsidized, private social benefits. For example, in the United Kingdom and Canada, private pensions and subsidized private savings similar to 401Ks and IRAs (Individual Retirement Accounts) are a major source of economic security for many workers and their families. Like in the United States, these private schemes often benefit middle-class and wealthier citizens rather than the poor, who rely more on social assistance and other direct public provisions (Howard 2006).

This prominent role of private benefits has stimulated the development of a growing comparative literature on the public–private dichotomy in social policy. This literature includes qualitative case studies and large-N quantitative analyses (e.g., Rein and

Rainwater 1986; Seeleib-Kaiser 2008; Shalev 1996); it also recognizes the intricate nature of the boundaries between public and private policy arrangements (Béland and Gran 2008; Rein and Schmähl 2004; Stevens 1988). The story about complex public–private boundaries in social policy has two major aspects.

First, the distinction between public and private schemes is frequently blurred because private benefits seldom exist in a legal and fiscal vacuum – the state can actively promote, regulate, and/or limit the expansion of private benefits (Gran 2003; Hacker 2002; Howard 1997; Stevens 1988). Even in policy areas where private institutions play the dominant role, the state generally sets the basic rules according to which these actors must operate. In many circumstances, state regulations are tied to major fiscal incentives that the state uses to subsidize the development of private benefits. This practice is found not only in liberal welfare regime countries such as the United States, Canada, and the United Kingdom but also in countries as different as Germany and even social-democratic Sweden.[5]

Second, private actors can play a key role in the management and distribution of public benefits and services (Gilbert 2002). For example, in recent decades, governments have been increasingly eager to contract out the delivery of a wide range of social services. In addition, private financial institutions can play a significant role in the administration of public retirement savings programs, which allow individuals to invest at least some of their contribution money in equity, a practice found in countries as different as Chile and Sweden (Béland and Gran 2008). The idea of public–private partnerships in a wide range of policy domains has also become increasingly popular since the 1980s, although these explicit partnerships have made it increasingly hard to draw a clear line between public and private social policy (Vaillancourt Rosenau 2000). Finally, non-profit organizations belonging to the community sector are directly involved in the provision of social services, sometimes with the support of public agencies (Jenson 2004).

The typically complex nature of public–private arrangements leads us to adopt a more careful approach to contemporary debates on welfare state privatization. Although this term is relevant in an era where firms attempt to shift financial risks onto workers and some politicians are tempted to increase the role of private actors in key policy areas (Hacker 2004), students of social policy must define what they mean by privatization. For example, in the United States, the term "privatization" refers to the idea of transforming at least part of the Social Security program into a set of personal savings accounts (Altman 2005; Edwards 2007). But, although this move would favor an individualization of protection while reducing the economic security of future retirees (Hacker 2006), it is the federal government that would provide the basic framework for the creation and the regulation of personal savings accounts (Béland 2005).

Importantly, in developed societies, the state can seldom withdraw entirely from a policy area, which is what the most radical interpretation of privatization would entail. Elected officials face intense pressure from the general public and specific interest groups alike to protect them against economic uncertainty and correct highly visible "market failure" (Jacobs and Teles 2007). But privatization does occur and, in order to understand it, it is necessary to account for the generally complex relationship between public and private interventions in developed societies, where the state plays a role in almost every aspect of economic and social life. From family law to tax policy and financial regulations, the state remains a central figure, even in the context of privatization and public–private partnerships. This does not mean that giving a greater role to the private sector is inconsequential; it only points to the fact that the state can play a major role in operating and regulating this transfer. In other words, the manner in which states decide to regulate private social provisions can shape their impact on economic insecurity and social inequality (Béland and Gran 2008).

In the United States, the strong reliance on publicly subsidized yet loosely regulated private benefits has reinforced, rather than mitigated, existing forms of social inequality (e.g., Hacker 2004; Howard 2006; Klein 2003; Quadagno 2005; Stevens 1988). This is clearly the case in the field of health-care, where disparities in private insurance coverage are a major source of inequality (Ruggie 1996; Street 2008). Importantly, however, in countries that rely massively on private health insurance, it is still possible to impose universal coverage, through mandates and other forms of state intervention and regulation. For example, as suggested above, in Switzerland, private health insurance remains dominant but coverage is universal (Bertozzi and Gilardi 2008). In the United States, the adoption of insurance mandates as part of the 2010 health-care reform discussed in Chapter 5 should significantly increase the level of health insurance coverage. To assess the impact of private benefits on social inequality, we must look at the level of state regulation. In itself, extensive reliance on private social policy is not necessarily a source of widespread inequality because the state has the power to reduce coverage gaps and other forms of inequality through comprehensive regulation (Gran and Béland 2008).

However, in the American context at least, strong reliance on voluntary, tax-subsidized pensions and savings schemes like IRAs (Individual Retirement Accounts) increases social inequality. As Jacob Hacker (2004) notes: "Tax breaks for private pensions and other retirement savings options heavily favor better paid employees: Two-thirds of the nearly $100 billion in federal tax breaks for subsidized retirement savings options accrue to the top 20% of the population" (p. 255). In the field of old-age security and beyond, the federal government is heavily subsidizing private social benefits that contribute directly to the reproduction of social inequality in terms of class, but also ethnicity, race, and gender. (These benefits are often less accessible to minorities and to the many women who work part-time.) Overall, the reliance of the United States on loosely regulated private benefits and regressive tax subsidies contributes to its higher levels of poverty and income inequality in comparison to most other developed societies (Howard 2006).

Beyond their relationship to social inequality, private benefits and the tax policies promoting them are decades-old political constructions that have created powerful constituencies and institutions, which can make it harder for policymakers to reverse or alter the course of these constructions because so many actors believe it is in their interest to preserve them (Hacker 2002; Klein, 2003). From employers to private insurance companies, many interest groups are willing to fight to defend and even expand existing tax advantages that promote their perceived short-term economic interests. Additionally, wealthier citizens who benefit from regressive tax incentives are likely to oppose a new course of action that involves more progressive tax and social policies. Finally, poorer citizens and advocacy groups representing them, who might be willing to fight for change, are not necessarily aware of the sheer scope of the regressive components of what has been labeled "the hidden welfare state" (Howard 1997). Although countries like New Zealand have found a way to abolish well-rooted tax subsidies to private social policy schemes (Ashton and St John 2008), this type of fiscal policy typically creates powerful vested interests that can make radical political change affecting that policy less likely (Béland and Gran 2008; Hacker 2002).

In the United States, because many of the tax and regulatory policies that promote the development of private social benefits are relatively little known by the public, politicians have found it easier to expand tax and savings programs that favor wealthier citizens (Hacker 2004). And, because the public–private mix is often complex (Gran 2003), it is more difficult for citizens to learn who is accountable for this development of private but, at the same time, state-subsidized benefits that may only profit a privileged minority of the population. The political dimension of the public–private mix is critical for constructing a more informed debate on private benefits and their relationship to low-profile political decisions that shape their development and related patterns of social inequality.

Federalism and Territorial Inequalities

The distinction between unitary and federal states is a major institutional distinction in the world of social policy. Intriguingly, as opposed to the public–private policy mix, this distinction does not feature prominently in the welfare regime literature, even though countries belonging to the same welfare regime can have totally different forms of territorial organization. For instance, within the liberal regime, New Zealand is a unitary state, while the United States and Canada are federal systems. Consequently, in terms of the territorial nature of the welfare state, federalism is a crucial factor in North America and, compared to unitary countries such as France and Japan, the United States and Canada are characterized by more decentralized welfare states. Although forms of policy decentralization exist everywhere, federal states are distinct from unitary states due to the very nature of their institutional and constitutional order. In general, as an institutional principle, federalism

> organizes a division of sovereignty by creating several orders of government to coexist within the same political system. The federal principle . . . symbolizes a form of political integration based on a bond at once voluntary and restrictive, between several regional territorial entities, a bond that, in spite of the fragmentation of the political [order], will remain unified on a much larger scale. (Théret 1999: 480)

Under some circumstances, political tensions within federal systems can lead to secessionist attempts, as in the United States during the Civil War (1861–5). More recently, Belgium and Canada, both federal countries, have faced the threat of secession. In 1995, for example, the Canadian province of Quebec held a referendum that could have led to the separation of the French-speaking province from the rest of the country. The separatist movement lost the referendum by a very slight margin. In the United States, the most noteworthy secessionist movements existing today are active in remote parts of the country – Alaska, Hawaii, and, more particularly, Puerto Rico (Barreto 2007).

From a comparative perspective, the most important thing to know about federalism is that its meaning varies a great deal from one federal country to another. In terms of legislative authority over social programs, Canada and, to a lesser extent, the United States are typically more decentralized than federal states such as Australia and Germany. In Germany, the federal government has

the sole power to enact social programs in areas such as health-
care, retirement security, unemployment, and welfare, while the
states (*Länder*) are primarily in charge of implementing policies
enacted at the federal level. In contrast, in the United States, the
states have full legislative control over workers' compensation and
play a key institutional role in policy fields ranging from health-
care to unemployment insurance and welfare reform (Obinger,
Leibfried, and Castles 2005a: 25). Not only do the states have
a great deal of autonomy in setting benefit levels and eligibility
criteria for Medicaid and the TANF (Temporary Aid to Needy
Families) program – despite the existence of federal mandates –
they also run the unemployment insurance programs, which is
why benefit levels vary from state to state. In the United States, the
field of retirement security is probably the most centralized social
policy area, as Social Security and SSI (Supplemental Security
Income) are purely federal programs. Consequently, authority
over these public pension programs is unified.[6]

Institutional differences between countries and between policy
areas within the same country, as well as changes that may take
place over time, make it impossible to draw general conclusions
about the overall impact of federalism on welfare state development. In other words, "federalism does *not* affect welfare states
uniformly across time and space" (Obinger, Leibfried, and Castles
2005a: 8). This statement about temporal variations is particularly applicable to the United States (Finegold 2005), where
social policy is typically much more centralized today than it was
a century ago. Before the 1930s, social policy reform occurred
mainly in the states; the federal government did not take a central
role in that policy area until the New Deal. During the New Deal
years and the post-World War II era, the United States witnessed
a gradual yet incomplete process of institutional centralization,
which increased the role of the federal government in American
society. This process culminated in the 1960s and the early 1970s.
For example, in 1972, social assistance for the disabled and the
elderly was centralized with the adoption of the above-mentioned
SSI program (Berkowitz 1991).

Conservative attempts to decentralize social policy by reducing

the number of federal mandates and regulations (Conlan
have been largely unsuccessful, with the result that the welfare
state remains more centralized there than in some other federal
countries. For example, the Canadian welfare state is more decentralized on average than its American counterpart, partly because
of the strength of political regionalisms and partly because the
ten provinces are constantly involved in direct policy discussions
with the central government, notably through federal–provincial
meetings (Théret 2002). The contrast between Canada and the
United States illustrates cross-national institutional differences
that characterize the territorial politics of the welfare state
(Maioni 1998).

Although, as noted above, such differences make it difficult
to generalize about the impact of federalism on the welfare state
(Obinger, Leibfried, and Castles 2005b), examining the key
features of American federalism that relate to welfare state development is still useful. First, compared to other federal countries,
the United States has a stronger emphasis on economic and fiscal
competition between the states (Obinger, Leibfried, and Castles
2005a: 10). Unlike both Australia and Canada, the United States, a
member of the liberal welfare regime, does not have a large, stand-
alone fiscal equalization program for reducing fiscal disparities
between poorer and wealthier states (Théret 1999). The absence of
such a program intensifies the fiscal competition between the fifty
American states, and it may lead them to participate in a "race to
the bottom" as they are under pressure to control or even reduce
their social expenditures in order to stay competitive in terms of
their tax levels (Finegold 2005; Peterson 1995). In this context,
policy decentralization can have conservative consequences, as
states push to reduce spending and tax rates to compete with their
neighbors for jobs and investments. Although there is no international consensus on the systematic presence of a race to the bottom
in decentralized policy areas (Noël 1999), in the United States at
least, fiscal competition between states remains fierce, a situation
that has negative consequences for state-level policy development.
Yet, even in the United States, decentralization can stimulate the
diffusion of policy experiments that may subsequently lead to an

expansion of social protection rather than a race to the bottom (Finegold 2005).

A second key feature of American federalism involves racial inequality. For decades, the push to maintain or increase social policy decentralization in the federal system was related to attempts on the part of Southern elites to both control and exclude African Americans living in their states. During the New Deal era, when the federal welfare state began to emerge, Southern Democrats in Congress successfully pushed for more lenient federal standards in the field of social assistance (Lieberman 1998; Quadagno 1988), and the decision to adopt weak federal standards as part of the 1935 Social Security Act allowed Southern states to preserve much of their autonomy in the administration of social assistance programs. Thus, in a context of deeply rooted racism and segregation, state officials could discriminate against African Americans and exclude them from benefits. This overly racist social assistance model only collapsed in the 1960s, as a consequence of the civil rights movement (Quadagno 1994). Overall, from a historical standpoint, there is a close relationship between racial inequality and the politics of federalism in the United States (Lieberman 1998).

A third key feature concerns welfare reform. Although conservatives have generally promoted more limited federal government involvement in social policy, in the United States, as elsewhere, centralization is not always synonymous with welfare state expansion. For example, as mentioned in Chapter 1, the 1996 welfare reform not only limited federal spending by replacing matching federal funds with block grants, it also imposed country-wide time limits that effectively ended welfare as a guaranteed entitlement. In other words, rather than letting state governments set their own basic entitlement standards, American conservatives and their allies used the federal government to impose their vision of "work ethics" across the nation (Waddan 2003; Weaver 2000). This example suggests that welfare state centralization – in this case, the imposition of new federal standards – can have regressive outcomes if it is inspired by conservative ideas. Contrary to a widely held common wisdom, conservatism can promote centralization and even "big government" when these approaches are consistent with other ideological imperatives like the promotion of ᶴ family or religious values (Béland and Vergniolle de Chantal ᴢᴜᴜ⸍,. Alternatively, in developed societies such as the United States, decentralization can acquire a progressive meaning when principles like local democracy and community empowerment guide policy change. In fact, it is possible to imagine forms of decentralization that help expand social protection (Noël 1999). In the United States, the Office of Economic Opportunity, created in the 1960s and discussed in Chapter 3, is a fine example of decentralized, yet progressive, social policy. Thus, in that country, the use by conservative forces of federalism and the defense of "state's rights" as devices to stimulate fiscal competition between states or, in the past, to preserve racial hierarchies does not mean that decentralization cannot take a progressive meaning. But in order to generate outcomes compatible with citizenship inclusion, decentralization must occur in a general fiscal and institutional context that is unlikely to transform devolution into a race to the bottom (Théret 1999).

This discussion on federalism and decentralization suggests that students of the welfare state should pay direct attention to territorial issues, especially as they relate to social inequality. Understanding the nature of territorial inequalities as they intersect with issues of race, economic development, and political institutions is a primary task of social policy research, both within and beyond federal political systems. Even in unitary states, the territorial aspect of social inequality can become a serious policy concern. For example, in France, a well-known social and territorial gap exists between cities like Paris and poor suburbs where immigrants and their families are overrepresented, and this gap is a source of resentment and violent protest for marginalized suburban youth (Béland and Hansen 2000). This type of territorial inequality between urban and suburban settings takes on a different meaning in the United States, where inner cities tend to be poorer than suburbs. Rural poverty in the United States, as elsewhere, is another major social problem, one that does not currently receive much media attention. But back in the early 1960s, Michael Harrington's influential book *The Other America* (1962) exposed the fact that poverty in rural regions such as

Appalachia represented a huge policy challenge and a source of legitimate moral outrage. Moreover, although policies have been enacted to fight rural poverty, it remains a significant yet lower-profile problem to this day. For instance, the national media have devoted a great deal of attention to the impact of the 1996 welfare reform on the urban poor, while generally neglecting the rural poor. Under most circumstances, poor people living in rural areas face limited access to educational and work opportunities, which makes it particularly difficult for them to improve their living standards (Pickering et al. 2006). The plight of the rural poor is yet another example of why no serious student of the welfare state can or should ignore the fact that social inequality and related policy issues have critical territorial components.

Finally, a noteworthy, yet less-studied, component of the territorial dimension of the welfare state is the construction of national identities (Béland and Lecours 2008; McEwen 2006). As discussed in Chapter 1, social programs, especially universal transfers and services, deal with citizenship and debates on identity, immigration, and membership. In countries such as Canada, the United Kingdom, and Sweden, where universal programs are well developed, the welfare state is explicitly construed as a primary source of political integration and national identity.[7] For instance, since the 1970s, universal health coverage has become a prominent symbol of national identity in Canada, which English-speaking Canadians use to emphasize the differences between their country and their powerful southern neighbor. Concretely, this means that many Canadians see universal health-care coverage as part of their national identity (Boychuk 2008; Brodie 2002). More generally, health and social policy is a major nation-building tool in Canada, a country in which the province of Quebec has created a distinct identity that clashes with the identity developed in English-speaking Canada (Banting 2005). In the United States, although a patriotic discourse at times surrounds Medicare and Social Security, the relationship between national identity and the welfare state is mainly apparent with issues related to military service, such as the GI Bill. The weaker relationship between national identity and the welfare state in the United States is probably related to its traditional lack of universal transfers and services, as well as to the strength of its constitutional patriotism. Indeed, the American national creed seems more robust than that of territorially divided countries like Belgium, Canada, or even the United Kingdom, where nationalists in places like Scotland emphasize their own national and territorial identity over British identity and the central state (Béland and Lecours 2008; McEwen 2006). Overall, it is important to recognize that, because social programs are often related to issues like citizenship and solidarity, they can play a role in the construction of territorial and national identities.

Conclusion

Through a discussion of the concept of welfare regime that is found in the growing international literature on this topic, this chapter has enhanced our comparative understanding of American social policy. Knowing the nature of the liberal welfare regime as defined by Esping-Andersen is an effective way to place the United States in its international context, even though his welfare regime typology suffers from a number of flaws, especially concerning gender as well as ethnic and race relations. In order to shed some light on social inequality and institutional fragmentation within and beyond the liberal welfare regime, the discussion then turned to the complex and changing relationship between public and private benefits. The final section of the chapter explored another form of policy fragmentation: federalism and territorial inequalities within and between countries. Interestingly, territorial inequalities are related to the public–private dichotomy because both public and private social coverage in fields can vary a great deal from one state or region of the country to another. For example, in the United States in the late 2000s, the percentage of the population living without health insurance was much higher in Texas than in Hawaii or Massachusetts.[8] In the next chapter, we will further locate issues such as health-care coverage in their broad historical and political contexts by discussing theories of welfare state development and their application to the American case.

3

Welfare State Development

A century ago, retirement was not a widespread institution in the United States. At the time, only a small percentage of employers offered pensions to their elderly workers. In many cases, people would work until they faced disability or death. Today, many of us would find this situation unacceptable, but this is how our ancestors lived and died. It was only during the Great Depression that, in a context of extreme economic insecurity, Congress enacted Social Security, a program that later helped transform retirement into a key institution in American society (Graebner 1980). In the United States as in other countries, the development of public pension programs like Social Security has transformed our lives in such a way that we may find it hard to imagine the world without them.

As this example suggests, social programs that shape the lives of millions of people today are the product of a long history, which usually featured unexpected twists and turns. As the welfare regime literature suggests, welfare state development has never been about the linear expansion of a universal social model that remains basically the same in every country. Indeed, although institutional convergence occurred in some policy areas, cross-national variations in policy design remained strong throughout the post-World War II era, during which a general trend toward welfare state expansion took a specific form in each country. Building on the basic historical information on specific programs provided in the previous two chapters, it is now time to take a more systematic look at the history of the welfare state.

Recognizing that it is impossible to fully explore the complex history of modern welfare states in such a short book, this chapter simply sketches a general overview of the historical development of modern social programs in developed countries. Focusing on the United States, the chapter explores key moments in modern welfare state development from the late 1800s to the 1970s. In addition to providing the basic timeline for the emergence of modern social programs, the chapter reviews political and sociological theories of welfare state development. Among other things, each of these theories is an attempt to explain the major cross-national differences that characterize modern welfare state development. Following the lead of John Myles and Jill Quadagno (2002), it is argued that these distinct theories can frequently complement one another in explaining dominant historical and political episodes.

For the sake of clarity, the chapter is divided into two main sections. The first section relates the basic story of welfare state development in Europe, followed by a more detailed discussion of the American case. Beginning with Europe is crucial partly because many early American reformers looked at Europe for reform ideas that they later adapted to the New World context (Moss 1995; Rodgers 2000). The second section discusses four main theories of welfare state development – industrialism, the power resource approach, historical institutionalism, and the cultural and ideational perspective – in order to shed light on historical and institutional differences between the United States and other developed countries. To make the historical narration more straightforward, the chapter focuses primarily on public social benefits while referring to the development of private schemes when appropriate.

Social Policy History

The European Experience

The early nineteenth-century British debate on the future of the Poor Law has been described as a defining moment in the emergence of modern social policy (Castel 2003; Polanyi 2001; Somers and Block 2005). To understand this debate, we can turn to Karl Polanyi's book *The Great Transformation*. In his book, Polanyi (2001) illustrates how in early nineteenth-century England the push to create a modern capitalist labor market led to the dismantling of the Speenhamland Law, a paternalistic law aimed at preventing the crystallization of a modern labor market in which, as opposed to the then prevailing feudal system, workers would be free to sell their labor to potential employers. Enacted in 1795 to provide a minimum income to the poor "irrespective of their earnings," the Speenhamland Law supported both the jobless and the working poor (p. 82). However, according to Polanyi, the law had perverse economic effects as it reduced work incentives and labor productivity while encouraging employers to offer low wages:

> Under the Speenhamland Law a man was relieved even if he was in employment, as long as his wages amounted to less than the family income granted to him by the scale. Hence, no laborer had any financial interest in satisfying his employer, his income being the same whatever wages he earned. . . . Within a few years the productivity of labor began to sink to that of pauper labor, thus providing an added reason for employers not to raise wages above the scale. (p. 83)

Given this situation, proponents of economic liberalism called for the dismantlement of the Speenhamland system and the creation of what they imagined to be a self-regulated labor market, whereby the state would stop supporting the working poor. These proponents of economic liberalism believed that the protection of individual rights, especially private property, should become the foundation of a new system of economic regulation in which the state would only perform a small number of basic tasks, such as policing and national defense. In 1834, they achieved their goal through the successful enactment of the Poor Law Reform, which abolished financial support for the working poor and forced poor people seeking social assistance to enter the poorhouse, an institution that carried tremendous stigma in nineteenth-century British society. More generally, by reducing the level of economic state intervention, the 1834 reform helped create "a competitive labor market . . . in England" (p. 87).

In the next decades, other countries followed Britain's lead by creating competitive labor markets associated with economic liberalism. Although these markets appeared to be self-regulated, massive state intervention was still necessary to eliminate the legacies of feudalism that stood in the way of economic individualism and of the related diffusion of the capitalist labor contract (Polanyi 2001). To a large extent, the first modern social programs and labor laws to be adopted, starting in the late nineteenth century, were a response to the dire consequences of economic liberalization for industrial workers, who typically faced high levels of poverty and economic insecurity in a context of rapid industrialization and urbanization (Castel 2003). The extreme deprivation faced by industrial workers who, with their families, subsisted in unsanitary slums was described – and denounced – by Karl Marx and other nineteenth-century European thinkers and activists (Woodall 2005).

Yet, interestingly, the goal of the first modern social programs in Europe was not to empower workers to force radical social change but rather to reinforce the existing social and political order by providing some economic security to wage workers. In late nineteenth-century Germany, for instance, Otto von Bismarck created the first modern social insurance schemes largely to weaken support for the socialist movement among workers by granting them access to – modest – social benefits (Abrams 2006: 40). At first, these schemes only targeted industrial workers, but they were later expanded to cover other occupational categories such as farmers, and until World War I, the German system, widely known as the "Bismarckian model" (i.e., the primacy of occupational social insurance schemes), influenced other European countries to enact their own social insurance schemes. Although limited in scope and coverage, these schemes helped propagate the idea of social insurance, which emerged as an alternative to the voluntarist and self-reliance creed that had failed to adequately protect the majority of wage workers against poverty and economic insecurity (Ewald 1986). Following World War I and during the Great Depression, new social reforms expanded the safety net in many European countries. However, with a few exceptions, universal coverage and extensive state protection for all citizens rarely emerged as a key political priority before World War II; instead, countries such as Belgium, France, and Germany remained faithful to the occupational segmentation of social insurance associated with the Bismarckian model that is at the heart of what would later be known as the modern conservative welfare regime (Baldwin 1990; Esping-Andersen 1990).

An alternative to that social insurance model emerged during World War II. At the same time as Britain was at war with Nazi Germany, the British government commissioned a series of reports that paved the way for post-war reforms aimed at helping both reconstruct the country and improve the social and economic life of its citizens. The content of these reports, however, can only be understood in the context of World War II, a time in which the sense of national solidarity among British citizens was heightened, given the common threat of Nazi invasion they faced (Titmuss 1963b).[1] The most influential of these documents is the 1942 report *Social Insurance and Allied Services*, by economist and civil servant William Beveridge, who proposed the creation of a universalistic welfare state that would cover the British population as a whole against major modern economic and social risks. Immediately after the war, the Labour government of Clement Attlee (1945–51) enacted bold reforms that created programs such as the National Health Service, which granted access to health-care services to all British citizens (Glennerster 2000), and these reforms embodied what became known as the "Beveridge model," which stressed the need for universal, state-granted social protection (Bonoli 1997).

Although in his 1942 report Beveridge had focused on the key role of flat social insurance contributions, the model named after him became synonymous with a type of egalitarian universalism that emerged as an alternative to the Bismarckian model, which has remained dominant in European countries such as Belgium, France, and Germany. In some of these countries, attempts to implement the Beveridge model failed because occupational groups fought to preserve the autonomy of their social insurance schemes (Baldwin 1990). As for the Scandinavian countries, they built on earlier reforms to create a more radical version of the Beveridge model, a version embedded in the growth of universal transfers and services that became a central feature of the social-democratic welfare regime (Esping-Andersen, 1990).

Overall, the post-war era witnessed the expansion of European welfare states, with the state playing a growing role in economic regulation. Inspired by the work of economist John Maynard Keynes, this statist approach to economic regulation moved away from traditional economic liberalism and gave a positive meaning to the expansion of the modern welfare state, which, in the end, became part of a broader model of state intervention in social and economic affairs. However, despite the international domination of the Keynesian approach and the general trend toward welfare state expansion in Western Europe, differences between national social-policy systems were evident throughout the post-war era (Esping-Andersen 1990). Developed countries all experienced welfare state expansion in a context of economic growth and Keynesian support for statist economic regulation, but these shared trends did not lead to a strong form of institutional convergence. Thus, although common trends like the expansion of social benefits existed across the developed world, they did not eliminate major differences in policy settings, ranging from benefit levels to eligibility criteria, and in state support for private social programs.

Welfare regime typologies like Esping-Andersen's (1990) are attempts to make sense of the enduring institutional diversity of the modern national social policy systems that were created during the post-war era. At the same time, these attempts should not preclude us from noting what is specific about each country. For instance, Canada and the United States, both federal countries described as belonging to the liberal welfare regime, are quite different from one another – at least in some policy areas such as health-care (Boychuk 2008; Maioni 1998). At the most general level, knowing the history of social programs in other countries is crucial for understanding the distinct aspects of welfare state development in the United States. Before we consider theories of welfare state development that may explain such distinct aspects, we will review a few key moments in the history of the American welfare state. This brief and necessarily superficial overview will help to identify some of the key historical differences between the United States and other developed countries.

The American Experience

As in Europe, welfare state development in the United States is not about the gradual expansion of a coherent and universal model that would face more obstacles in some countries or policy areas than in others. Instead, the history of American social policy is, like that of other nations, full of unpredictable twists and false starts. Although a short overview such as this cannot explain these in detail,[2] it is sufficient to suggest that in the United States, as elsewhere, welfare state development is seldom a linear process.

Economic liberalism and the idea of laissez-faire dominated American economic and social debate in the decades following the Civil War (Fine 1956). At that time, the federal government had no major role in social policy; as for the states, although they were active in fields such as education reform and labor legislation, before the early twentieth century, their welfare involvement remained limited to issues of charity boards and pensions for the blind (Eldersveld 2007: 74–5). Social assistance for the poor, an area in which local governments and voluntary organizations had long played a dominant role, remained the central focus of social policy. In the nineteenth century, as in Britain, the poorhouse was a key aspect of the social assistance system, although by the mid-nineteenth century, instead of caring for the socially and physically disadvantaged under one roof, more specialized institutions had emerged to take care of specific populations: "Specialized institutions had been founded to care for the mentally ill, to rehabilitate juvenile delinquents, to educate the blind, deaf, and dumb, and to eradicate ignorance" (Katz 1996: 11). As for outdoor relief (i.e., social benefits available to the poor outside the poorhouse), just as in Britain during the debate on the Speenhamland Law, it came under growing attack during the mid to late nineteenth century (Pimpare 2004: 82–5). This campaign against outdoor relief, which was related to an attempt by the "respectable classes" to prevent the emergence of "a united, militant working class," resulted in an overall decline of the local support available to the poor outside institutions of direct social control, such as the poorhouses (Katz 1996: 113).

In the last decade of the nineteenth century and the first decade of the twentieth, the social policy debate in the United States underwent a transformation, stemming from the growing influence of the progressive movement and its push for broad economic, moral, and social reforms.[3] To fight corruption and to solve social problems resulting from processes such as industrialization, immigration, and urbanization, progressives reframed the policy agenda in ways that tended to legitimize greater state intervention in the American economy and society. A fascinating episode of the Progressive Era was the attempt by the American Association for Labor Legislation (AALL) to adapt European social insurance ideas for the United States (Moss 1995).

From the late nineteenth century onward, a growing number of American reformers and government officials began studying the first modern social programs enacted in countries such as Great Britain, France, and Germany (Rodgers 2000). In a letter to the State Department written in February 1881, the American Ambassador to Germany, Andrew White, informed his government of the social insurance reforms recently launched by Chancellor Otto von Bismarck (cited in DeWitt, Béland, and Berkowitz 2007: 35–6). During the following two decades, detailed studies of European social insurance began to appear in the United States (e.g., Brooks 1893; Franklin 1898), but it took the creation of the AALL in 1906 to stimulate the emergence of a home-grown American social insurance movement (Moss 1995).

In the 1910s, however, the AALL's state-level campaigns for social insurance had mixed success (Moss 1995; Skocpol 1992). On one hand, during the 1910s, this association successfully promoted its social insurance model in the workers' compensation debate; by 1920, more than forty states had adopted social insurance compensation schemes to cover victims of work-related accidents and their families (Lubove 1968). On the other hand, in the fields of health and unemployment insurance, similar state-level campaigns failed miserably, and no state enacted either type of program during the 1910s (Lubove 1968; Nelson 1969; Numbers 1978; Skocpol 1992). Strong opposition from the business community, which was made more effective by the fragmented logic of American federalism, largely explains the political defeat of health and unemployment insurance campaigns before the Great Depression (Hacker and Pierson 2002).

Clearly, most social insurance initiatives during the Progressive Era failed (Moss 1995). However, beginning in the late nineteenth century, significant forms of social policy expansion did take place. Specifically, as Theda Skocpol noted in her 1992 book *Protecting Soldiers and Mothers*, two types of programs expanded: military pensions and new social assistance programs designed to help poor mothers and their children. Legislation enacted from the 1860s into the 1900s considerably enlarged the federal military pensions for Civil War Union veterans and their families. Although many Confederate veterans received state benefits, federal pensions available only to Union veterans were much higher on average, a situation that shaped the territorial distribution of pension money (Quadagno 1988). By 1910, in the country at large, veteran pensioners made up nearly a third "of all American men over age sixty-five" (Orloff 1993a: 136), but the system soon began to decline as veterans and war widows gradually passed away. In the end, as Skocpol (1992) points out, military pensions did not lead to the creation of a permanent civilian pension system, partly because many reformers thought military pensions were directly related to patronage (i.e., the allocation of government jobs and resources based on political connections), which came under attack before and especially during the Progressive Era.

Reformers and advocates also successfully promoted the development of state-level mothers' pensions throughout the Progressive Era and the 1920s (Skocpol 1992). Modest in scope, these social assistance benefits became a source of stigma for beneficiaries and, under many circumstances, a tool of social control aimed at poor and minority women (Gordon 1994). Although organizations representing women played an instrumental role in bringing about these mothers' pensions (Skocpol 1992), they generally remained modest in scope (Gordon 1994), at least compared to some European social insurance programs, which, in the first decades of the twentieth century, targeted wage workers, who at the time were mostly male breadwinners. Overall, there is no doubt that the social policy reforms that took place during and after the Progressive Era were gendered in nature (Gordon 1994; Skocpol 1992).

The progressive and reformist impetus declined during the prosperous 1920s, but the Great Depression unexpectedly crushed the American economy. Between 1929 and 1933, for instance, investment fell by nearly 100 percent and GDP by almost 30 percent (McElvaine 1984: 75). At the peak of the Depression, when more than one American adult out of four was unemployed (Bernstein 1985: 21), many citizens faced profound deprivation related to the absence of a safety net comparable to the one available at the time in some other industrial nations (Béland 2005). Although states developed social assistance programs in response to the crisis, they faced major fiscal constraints that increased the need for federal intervention, and calls for the federal government to play a greater role in social and economic policy became increasingly louder (Amenta 1998; Bernstein 1985; Skocpol 1995).

Once elected, to help the jobless and pump up the economy, Democratic president Franklin Delano Roosevelt (1933–45) pushed for bold economic and social reforms. Although explicitly rejecting socialism, Roosevelt's discourse called for a much greater role for the state in the lives of citizens. The strong Democratic majorities in Congress allowed Roosevelt to push an ambitious policy agenda that attempted to rescue capitalism by reforming it through direct federal intervention. In terms of social policy, many of his early initiatives focused on public works projects rather than permanent social programs like social insurance ones (Amenta 1998). Designed as temporary programs, these initiatives became the central source of federal social assistance during the New Deal (Bremer 1975). As a result, federal social spending rose after Roosevelt took office in 1933. In fact, five years later, the

United States was spending more on social programs as a proportion of GDP than were France and Great Britain (Amenta 1998: 5) – countries that had enacted major national social programs several decades before the United States. The temporary nature of the public works programs partly responsible for this increase in federal social spending nevertheless meant they would be phased out as soon as prosperity returned to the country, which is exactly what happened when it finally did (Amenta 1998).

Beyond these bold initiatives that provided employment to millions of jobless Americans during the Great Depression, the New Deal witnessed the creation of permanent social programs that helped restructure the American economy and increase the role of the federal government in American society (Béland 2005). Interestingly, although it considerably expanded the role of the federal government, the 1935 Social Security Act only featured one purely federal program (old-age insurance, known today as Social Security). The other provisions of this legislation included new grants-in-aid to the states for social assistance and a 3 percent employer contribution that was a strong incentive for the states to adopt their own unemployment insurance programs, because only states that did so received the money collected in their jurisdiction through the new federal contribution. By the summer of 1937, all the states had adopted an unemployment insurance program (Skocpol 1995: 170).

Social Security was not meant to offer short-term relief, since the federal government planned to allocate the first pension benefits in 1942, seven years after legislation was enacted. However, in 1939, amendments to the act expanded the program and made benefits available as early as 1940 (Berkowitz 1983). In addition to pressure from Republicans, who criticized the anticipated size of the Social Security trust fund, the growing influence of the Townsend Plan helped justify the enactment of the 1939 amendments (Amenta 2006). Formulated in the mid-1930s, the Townsend Plan proposed that the federal government offer much larger old-age pensions in order to stimulate the economy, a proposal that was supported by millions of elderly Americans. Although few economists and elected officials took the policy ideas of this social movement very seriously, it added an element of political urgency to pension reform in the late 1930s (Amenta 2006). This type of grass-roots movement became common during the New Deal era, as an increasing number of citizens looked to the federal government for support in a context of enduring economic and social deprivation (Piven and Cloward 1971).

The social programs created by the New Deal did not, however, strongly challenge existing forms of gender and racial inequality, as social policy efforts focused mainly on male workers, on the assumption that most women and children depended on them for their survival. Indeed, there is strong evidence that traditional gender roles directly influenced major policy decisions adopted during the New Deal (Gordon 1994; Kessler-Harris 2001; Mettler 1998). The issue of race also influenced key policies such as social assistance programs. Because Southern Democrats played a major role within the "Roosevelt coalition," federal social programs created during the New Deal seldom challenged existing racial hierarchies, leaving Southern states free to pursue their openly racist and segregationist policies. In fact, many of these federal programs reinforced entrenched patterns of inequality (Brown 1999; Lieberman 1998; Quadagno 1988).[4] In the case of Social Security, for example, the exclusion of agricultural and domestic workers from coverage meant that millions of black and other minority workers did not participate in the program until these occupational categories finally gained coverage in the 1950s.[5]

In the United States, World War II brought a return to enduring economic prosperity that had remained elusive during the New Deal era. For instance, unemployment declined sharply after 1940 (Fite and Reese 1973). But, partly because the 1942 congressional election increased the weight of the Republican Party in Congress (Skocpol and Amenta 1988), path-breaking social policy reforms did not move to the center of the federal policy agenda, with the exception of the GI Bill (the 1944 Servicemen's Readjustment Act), which focused on military personnel and their families (Mettler 2005). In the civilian world, the publication of major federal reports and even William Beveridge's war-time visit to the United States (Altmeyer 1965) could not counter trends like the growing influence of the conservative coalition in Congress, comprised of Republicans and Southern Democrats who opposed social policy expansion during and immediately after the war (Skocpol and Amenta 1988). In the late 1940s and early 1950s, the advent of the Cold War and McCarthyism further weakened the push for comprehensive reform, as many left-leaning ideas came under attack, as did the people who had embraced them (Schrecker 1998).

Yet despite these trends, as in other developed nations, the United States did witness welfare state expansion during the postwar era. Starting in the early 1950s, Social Security was expanded and a Disability Insurance program was created (Berkowitz 1987; Derthick 1979). Throughout this period, federal bureaucrats such as Wilbur Cohen and Robert Ball played a key role in the expansion of existing programs and the creation of new policies (Berkowitz 1995, 2003). Under most circumstances, top federal bureaucrats adopted an incremental, long-term reform strategy to expand federal social programs (Derthick 1979; Tynes 1996), but in order to achieve their objectives, they needed support from congressional committees and their leaders (Béland 2005). During most of the post-war era, these committees and Democratic politicians like Arkansas Representative Wilbur Mills frequently promoted welfare state expansion (Zelizer 1998). Conversely, Republicans, as early as the Eisenhower years (1953–61), officially rallied behind popular programs such as Social Security while attempting to slow down welfare state expansion (Pratico 2001).

In addition to the incremental expansion of programs such as Social Security, private health and pension benefits witnessed much growth during the post-war era (Hacker 2002; Howard and Berkowitz 2008; Klein 2003; Quadagno 1988). Stimulated by labor mobilization in the industrial sector (e.g., the auto industry), this expansion generated a great deal of hope among workers and citizens but private health and pension schemes never came close to being universal in coverage (Klein 2003). Moreover, the relationship between public and private social benefits varied greatly from one policy area to another (Béland and Hacker 2004; Hacker 2002). In the field of old-age pensions, private benefits built on top of Social Security, which became the foundation of the American

Table 3.1   Selected key moments in the development of federal social programs (1935–75)

1935	Enactment of the Social Security Act (SSA), a federal bill featuring social assistance, unemployment insurance, and Social Security provisions
1939	1939 Amendments to the SSA create Social Security survivor benefits
1950	1950 amendments to the SSA begin post-war expansion of Social Security
1956	Disability insurance enacted as part of the 1956 amendments to the SSA
1964	Enactment of the Economic Opportunity Act (EOA) at the center of President Johnson's War on Poverty; creation of the Food Stamps program
1965	Enactment of Medicaid and Medicare
1972	Enactment of the Supplemental Security Income (SSI) program; Medicare expanded to cover disability insurance recipients
1975	Enactment of the Earned Income Tax Credit (EITC) program

pension system (apRoberts, 2000). Indeed, many employers came to see Social Security as a way to reduce their private pension costs (Hacker 2002). In the field of health-care, powerful interest groups such as the American Medical Association successfully mobilized against the advent of national health insurance during the Truman presidency (1945–53) and well beyond (Gordon 1997; Mayes 2004; Quadagno 2005). Here, the expansion of private health insurance benefits took the form of a perceived alternative to direct state intervention, a situation that did not really occur in the field of pension policy, where public and private pensions seemed to complement one another (Hacker 2002).[6]

For several reasons, the 1960s were a turning point for the emerging federal welfare state. First, the growing strength of the civil rights movement pushed the issue of desegregation and racial justice to the center of the federal policy agenda (for a nuanced view, see Davies 1996: 45). Second, a major debate on poverty emerged in a general context of economic prosperity, which suggested that poverty was a legacy of the past that the state should try to eliminate (Harrington 1962). Third, the assassination of

President John F. Kennedy in 1963, and the Democratic land-slide in Congress it helped to trigger a year later, empowered reformers wanting to expand the federal welfare state and largely explains why Congress passed both Medicare and Medicaid in 1965 (Marmor 2000; Oberlander 2003: 4). Fourth, to tackle poverty and racial inequality, President Lyndon Johnson (1965–9) launched his ambitious War on Poverty (Davies 1996). It featured large educational and community initiatives tied to the new Office of Economic Opportunity and the enactment of innovative pro-grams like Head Start and Food Stamps, which have remained key components of the American social assistance system (King 2000). Rapidly, however, the War on Poverty suffered from budget constraints related to the Vietnam War and became increasingly controversial in a context of urban riots and social discontent (Moynihan 1969). The debate on the alleged "failure" or "success" of the War on Poverty remains unsolved, an illustration of how welfare state history can become a contested political issue (Cazenave 2007; Murray 1994).

A vocal opponent of the War on Poverty, President Richard Nixon (1969–74) rejected the logic of community empowerment associated with it. The new Republican president put forward an alternative social assistance agenda centered on the idea of a guaranteed income for both the unemployed and the working poor. Partly because it included these two social categories within the same social assistance program, Nixon's initiative came under strong attack from the left and the right. As noted above, this was so because, while creating work incentives for the disadvantaged, Nixon's proposal would have eliminated the distinction between the deserving and the undeserving poor that is so central to both American culture and existing social programs (Steensland 2007). In the end, the Nixon administration failed to convince Congress to adopt this proposal. Instead, during Nixon's presidency, Democrats in Congress successfully pushed for major benefit increases in Social Security (Derthick 1979; Weaver 1988). The enactment of the SSI (Supplemental Security Income) program in 1972 was a residue of Nixon's failed guaranteed income proposal but, as stated in Chapter 1, it concerned social assistance for the elderly and the disabled rather than for the working poor and unemployed single parents (Erkulwater 2006).

Although few people at the time could have anticipated this trend, the Nixon presidency represented the end of an era (Berkowitz 2006). As in other countries, the 1973 oil crisis and the stagflation of the mid- to late 1970s shifted American welfare state debates in a significant way, a story that will be told in Chapter 4. First, though, we must survey the theories of welfare state development that help make sense of the key cross-national differences that crystallized during the post-war era. Understanding the possible sources of these differences is the best way to shed historical and comparative light on the American case.

Theories of Welfare State Development

It is widely acknowledged that welfare state development in the United States lagged decades behind many European countries. In the field of old-age insurance, for example, the United States only adopted a national program (Social Security) in 1935, decades after countries like Germany and France (Orloff 1993a: 14). However, as noted earlier, social expenditures in the United States often exceeded European levels in the mid- to late 1930s, largely due to the massive public works initiatives that were launched as part of the New Deal (Amenta 1998). Compared to neighboring Canada, the United States continued to lead in some policy areas. For instance, Canada did not create an unemployment insurance system until the early 1940s – half a decade after the United States (Banting 1987) – and did not create an old-age insurance program until the mid-1960s (Boychuk and Banting 2008). It was only in the late 1950s and 1960s that the Canadian welfare state expanded to become more comprehensive on average than its American counterpart (Maioni 1998; Théret 2002).

Beyond the issue of timing, there are many other important questions at the center of the historical and sociological debate on welfare state development in the United States. Drawing upon comparative scholarship, these questions deal with issues such as the absence of universal public health-care coverage (Quadagno 2005) and the related reliance on tax-sponsored private health insurance (Hacker 2002). In response to these questions, scholars have developed sociological and political theories of welfare state development that are designed to help explain cross-national differences in social policy design. These theories, which are widely debated in the social science literature (e.g., Amenta, Bonastia, and Caren 2001; Béland and Hacker 2004; Béland and Shinkawa 2007; Myles and Quadagno 2002; O'Connor 2002; Skocpol 1992), help students of social policy grasp the main ways in which sociologists and political scientists explain historical trends and cross-national differences in welfare state development.[7]

The first of the four theories we will discuss is industrialism, a functionalist perspective that is grounded in the assumption that increases in social spending stem from economic and demographic changes (e.g., Kerr et al. 1960; Rimlinger 1971; Wilensky 1975). From this perspective, industrialization and related processes such as urbanization weaken the family as a traditional source of economic security while trends like population aging create new social needs. In this new economic and social environment, the theory claims, the state implements social programs in order to respond to these growing social needs. In other words, according to industrialism, there is a correlation between the welfare state, on one hand, and economic and demographic development, on the other. For Myles and Quadagno (2002), this is especially true about the strong version of the theory, which is grounded in the "implicit claim . . . that nations with comparable levels of economic development would converge at similar levels of welfare state development as well" (pp. 36–7).

Taken as a whole, industrialism is a useful approach because it is impossible to deny that factors like industrialization, urbanization, demographic aging, and the decline of the traditional – extended – family unit are instrumental in creating the economic and social demands that fuel welfare state expansion in developed societies (Myles and Quadagno 2002: 36). The problem, however, is that the theory of industrialism can hardly explain key variations in policy outcomes from one country to another, or even one policy area to another within the same country (Béland 2005; Skocpol 1992). For example, without turning to major political factors like the roles of institutions, interest groups, and political parties, it is hard to explain major cross-national differences between health-care systems (Maioni 1998).

The second theory, the power resource approach, is a far more politically centered perspective on welfare state development which focuses on labor mobilization rather than on general economic and demographic changes (e.g., Esping-Andersen 1985; Hicks 1999; Korpi 1983; Myles 1989; Stephens 1979). This approach is based on the idea of class struggle tied to the Marxist tradition, in the sense that the welfare state is depicted as the outcome of a political competition between capitalists and workers. But, as opposed to many traditional Marxists, power resource proponents believe in the capacity of the working class to use democratic means to increase their political influence and, in turn, improve their working conditions and their social and economic status. For the founders of the power resource approach, such as Gøsta Esping-Andersen (1985), Walter Korpi (1983), and John Stephens (1979), there is a direct relationship between the level and scope of social benefits and the political power of the labor movement, which is related to factors such as unionization rates and, more important, party representation. The contrast between post-war Sweden and the United States illustrates this basic argument. On one hand, in Sweden, where the labor movement was well organized politically and tied to a strong social-democratic party, the welfare state became highly comprehensive and featured higher levels of redistribution and citizenship inclusion. On the other hand, in the United States, where the labor movement was much weaker politically, the post-war welfare state was less redistributive and comparatively limited in scope. In this comparison, we can recognize the distinction between the social-democratic and the liberal welfare regime central to the work of Esping-Andersen (1990) discussed in Chapter 2. This is not accidental because this author is one of the founders of the power resource approach (Esping-Andersen 1985).

As far as labor power is concerned, the United States is a striking case. Unlike many European countries, the United States has no social-democratic or socialist party that focuses on promoting the perceived interests of the labor movement and, more generally, the working class (Lowi 1984; Sombart 1976). Historically, during and after the New Deal, the American labor movement forged an alliance with the Democratic Party, which has always drawn heterogeneous interest groups and regional factions and, as a result, it is only one of its major constituencies (Maioni 1998). This is in stark contrast to the situation in countries such as Belgium, Canada, Germany, Denmark, and Sweden, where genuine labor parties have appeared. In addition to Denmark and Sweden, where social-democratic parties largely dominated the post-war era (Korpi 1983), Canada witnessed the evolution of a major labor party during and immediately after the Great Depression; the party, known as the Co-operative Commonwealth Federation (CCF), was later replaced by the New Democratic Party (NDP). Although the CCF/NDP has never won a majority of votes at the federal level, it has exerted strong pressure by gaining power in a number of provinces and by becoming a key federal opposition party, and it also played a significant role in the development of national health insurance in Canada during the post-war era (Maioni 1998). In the absence of a similar social-democratic party, American post-war labor advocates were forced to fight within the Democratic Party to get their voice heard (Quadagno 1988).

The power resource approach does have shortcomings. One of them is the tendency of some power resource scholars to focus exclusively on the labor movement and disregard other forms of social mobilization that involve constituencies such as the elderly and the poor. In the American context, the examples of the Townsend Plan during the New Deal and the civil rights movement during the 1960s provide support for this claim (Amenta 2006; Piven and Cloward 1971). Another shortcoming of early power resource scholarship is the insufficient attention devoted to the impact of political institutions on labor power and political outcomes (Béland and Hacker 2004; Skocpol 1992). For example, the political parties mentioned above exist only in an institutional context specific to each polity. In general, institutions ranging from the Supreme Court to party systems impact the political strategies and the behavior of labor unions (Forbath 1991; Hattam 1993; Maioni 1998). Thus, when power resource scholars fail to recognize the role of political institutions, they are unable to account for some policy episodes and cross-national differences, something that recent power resource scholarship has recognized and sought to remedy (Huber and Stephens 2001).

The third major theory of welfare state development, which has become very influential since the 1980s, is known as historical institutionalism.[8] For this approach, political institutions and public policies create constraints and opportunities that impact the behavior of policy actors and, as a consequence, welfare state development (Amenta 1998; Béland 2005; Orloff 1993a; Skocpol 1992). To show how political institutions shape social policy decisions, proponents of this theory study how institutions allow or prevent specific social and political constituencies to impact policy through concrete opportunities and obstacles (Bonoli 2000; Immergut 1992; Kay 1999; Pierson 2001). For instance, in their provocative article "It's the Institutions, Stupid!," political scientists Sven Steinmo and Jon Watts (1995) argue that, in the United States, institutional factors such as checks and balances and lack of party discipline in Congress tend to empower interest groups that oppose bold reforms, such as the adoption of national health insurance.

Institutionalist scholars have also focused on the role of bureaucratic institutions in welfare state development. For example, Skocpol (1992) has argued that the comparatively slow development of modern – meritocratic – bureaucratic capacities in the context of American-style patronage became a significant obstacle to social policy expansion before the New Deal. These remarks stress the key role of bureaucratic processes in welfare state development (Heclo 1974; Marier 2005). Because of their complexity, modern social programs typically require significant administrative support. From this perspective, the welfare state is directly tied to the development of modern bureaucratic structures analyzed a century ago by Max Weber (1978).[9]

Beyond the role of bureaucratic and political institutions,

historical institutionalism points to the impact of what is known as "policy feedback," a concept that refers to the way in which past policy decisions create constituencies, incentives, and vested interests that are likely to impact future policy decisions (Pierson 1994; Skocpol 1992). For example, extensive programs like Medicare have created large constituencies that may support the program's expansion over time. From this perspective, programs can generate their own political support over time. Essentially, as the Medicare example suggests, the concept of policy feedback involves the dynamic nature of welfare state development and the general idea that "policy creates politics" (Lowi 1964).

Although insightful, historical institutionalism is not without limitations. First, in some instances, it can become an overly rigid framework that does not allow for even the possibility of major policy change without constitutional redesign. In their article noted above, Steinmo and Watts (1995) suggest that path-departing health-care reform is virtually impossible in the United States without the enactment of constitutional reform that would alter federal institutions to make them less susceptible to the influence of interest groups, among other things. This is a problematic argument (Béland and Waddan 2010b; Hacker 1997), especially in the aftermath of the 2009–10 health-care debate, which pointed to the institutional obstacles facing policymakers but also to the possibility of enacting large-scale health insurance reforms in the United States. Second, the concept of policy feedback and the idea that "policy creates politics," whereby social programs help shape constituencies and other vested interests that can later impact the political debates about their future, can leave little room for the possibility of bold policy change, at least when it is believed that existing policies have already created large constituencies that can mobilize to preserve them and defend the status quo (Campbell 2004; Hacker 2004; Streeck and Thelen 2005; Thelen 2003). Finally, institutional factors are necessary but hardly sufficient to explain patterns of welfare state development, both in the United States and abroad. "Although institutional analysis can tell us much about the *prospects* for reform, it does not generally provide sufficient explanations of the *content* of social legislation." (Béland and Hacker 2004: 52). Even if institutions can help shape the policy preferences of actors, on their own the beliefs and assumptions of those actors can have a strong impact on political decisions and policy outcomes (Blyth 2002; Campbell, 2004) – which leads us to our fourth approach to welfare state development: the cultural and ideational perspective.

This perspective is grounded in the assumption that the ways in which actors give meaning to their world can have a substantial impact on welfare state development. Somewhat less coherent than historical institutionalism or the power resource approach, the cultural and ideational perspective features two related streams: culturalism and ideational analysis.

Culturalist scholars argue that variations in national values explain key welfare state differences between countries (Levine 1988; Lipset 1990; Lubove 1968). Here, national values simply refer to shared cultural assumptions about the social and economic world that are the product of a specific national history. Nations see the world in specific ways that affect their social policy decisions (Levine 1988: 11). For example, it has been argued that the alleged domination of values like individualism and self-reliance has seriously constrained welfare state development in the United States (Lipset 1990; Lubove 1968). More recently, although they do not systematically focus on culture and national values, students of public opinion have highlighted the understudied impact of stable public preferences on welfare state development. For Clem Brooks and Jeff Manza (2007), public opinion that reflects the "embedded preferences" of a country's population explains cross-national social policy differences.

As for the ideational analysis stream, it stresses the role of ideas and related discursive processes in economic and social policy development (e.g., Béland and Cox 2010; Béland and Hacker 2004; Blyth 2002; Campbell 2004; Orloff and Palier 2009; Padamsee 2009; Schmidt 2010; Somers and Block 2005). In general, ideas refer to "claims about descriptions of the world, causal relationships, or the normative legitimacy of certain actions" (Parsons 2002: 48). Based on this definition, the concept of ideas is broader than that of national values, which focuses exclusively on shared normative beliefs (what is seen as "good" or "bad"). Peter Hall's work on policy paradigms illustrates the role of ideas in policymaking. For Hall (1993), a policy paradigm is a framework that spells out policy goals, policy problems, and the policy options aimed at addressing these problems (p. 279). An example of a policy paradigm is the workfare approach that directly impacted the 1996 federal welfare reform (Weaver 2000).

However, some cultural and ideational approaches have at least one major shortcoming: they can become so general in nature that concrete differences between and within countries become difficult to explain. At least, this is the case of culturalist arguments about national values. As Skocpol (1992) rightly argues, "Arguments about national values are too holistic and essentialist to give us the explanatory leverage we need to account for variations in the fate of different social policies, or for changes over time in the fate of similar proposals" (p. 17). For example, it is clear that a broad concept like "national values" cannot explain why countries adopt comprehensive policies in one policy area but far less comprehensive ones in another. For instance, Canada has adopted an inclusive, citizenship-based public health-care system while, in the field of old-age pensions, private benefits play a much greater role (Boychuk and Banting 2008). If we want to explain differences between these two policy areas, referring to broad national values is not useful because these are located at a level of reality that is too general to be of relevance. (By definition, national values are the same across policy areas.)

To address this type of criticism, sociologist Brian Steensland (2007) recently shifted the emphasis of culturalism away from the overly broad concept of national values by exploring the weight of "cultural categories," such as the opposition between deserving and undeserving poor in a specific policy area. From his perspective, "cultural categories" are better defined and more specific in nature than the so-called "national values," a vague concept that he avoids altogether. Interestingly, students of race and gender have long studied categories like male/female and black/white as well as related paradigms like "dependency" (Fraser and Gordon 1994). In the future, proponents of this type of cultural analysis could study how cultural categories facilitate change, rather than focusing on culture as an obstacle to path-departing reform, as Steensland does in his book.

Although most scholars view these four key theories of welfare state development as alternative explanations, it is not only possible but potentially useful to combine elements from these distinct theories to explain specific policy variations from one country to another and from one policy area – or one historical moment – to another within the same country (e.g., Béland and Shinkawa 2007; Huber and Stephens 2001; Iversen 2005; Myles and Quadagno 2002; Williamson and Pampel 1993). In the comparative literature on welfare state development, scholars have combined the close attention to political institutions associated with historical institutionalism with the focus on labor mobilization central to the power resource perspective (Huber and Stephens 2001). Another common combination is the articulation of historical institutionalism and the focus on the role of ideas in policy change (e.g., Béland and Hacker 2004; Campbell 2004; Hattam 1993; Parsons 2007; Schmidt 2010). Finally, regardless of their favorite approach, most students of welfare state development pay at least some attention to economic and demographic circumstances, which are at the core of industrialism (Myles and Quadagno 2002).

At the most general level, as Craig Parsons (2007) argues, combining insight from two or even more theoretical approaches is a potentially productive idea, as long as we clearly distinguish between the types of explanation we seek to combine. And yet, in social science analysis, simplicity remains a virtue, and combining distinct theoretical approaches is only suitable when there is strong evidence that none of the available stand-alone theories·is capable of explaining either a significant cross-national difference or an episode of policy change that needs to be accounted for (Parsons 2007).

When discussing the possibility of combining these four theoretical perspectives, it is essential to stress that, in their traditional form, they seldom emphasize the role of race and gender, which have become increasingly central to the contemporary social science literature on welfare state development. This does not mean that we must discard these theories altogether in order to bring gender and/or race to the forefront of the analysis. In fact, few students of race or gender would argue that race- or gender-centered approaches should replace traditional theories of welfare state development completely. Instead, these students commonly borrow from existing theories while systematically exploring how race and gender interact with other factors. In her 1988 work on the impact of race on the development of old-age pensions in the United States, far from focusing exclusively on race, Jill Quadagno employs the power resource approach to explore the role of labor alongside – and in relationship with – racial relations, especially the mobilization of Southern politicians against federal decisions that could advance the economic and social emancipation of African Americans. Robert Lieberman, in *Shifting the Color Line* (1998), borrows explicitly from historical institutionalism to stress the relationship between race and institutional design in American welfare state development. More recently, seeking to improve the institutionalist take on race and policy development, Lieberman (2005) makes use of the literature on ideas and policymaking.

To explain cross-national differences in policy design that shape gender relations, feminist scholars have taken into account insight from traditional theories of welfare state development. For instance, prominent American studies focusing on gender and welfare state development have borrowed extensively from historical institutionalism (Mettler 1998; Skocpol 1992). Furthermore, in the comparative literature on welfare state development, students of gender refer explicitly to cultural and ideational factors (Orloff and Palier, 2009), while some feminist scholars have focused exclusively on the interaction between gender relations and labor mobilization, the causal factors associated with the power resource perspective (Klein 2003). Finally, like other social policy scholars, students of gender consider economic and demographic changes that interact with both gender relations and welfare state development (O'Connor 2002).

Overall, scholars working on issues of gender and race have made a strong contribution to the contemporary theoretical debates on welfare state development by providing evidence that gendered and racial inequalities and power struggles can impact welfare state development. At the same time, in contemporary scholarship, gender and race appear as potential causal factors that can challenge or supplement traditional theories of welfare state development. In fact, these two factors typically encompass economic, power resource, institutional and/or cultural logics that interact in different ways depending on the context. In general, students of gender and race do not form two homogeneous groups, and their basic theoretical assumptions about the role of factors like ideas, institutions, and economic conditions vary greatly. Recognizing these differences is crucial to our understanding of existing historical accounts of the relationship between gender, race, and welfare state development in the United States and beyond.

Conclusion

Although attempting to summarize the history of modern welfare states in such a short book is not easy, this chapter provides some insight into the development of modern social policy in the United States and elsewhere. Clearly, a comparative and historical perspective is necessary to understand major characteristics of a country's welfare state, and the first section of the chapter, though superficial, does relate the broad historical trends witnessed from the nineteenth century to the 1970s. As for the theories of welfare state development discussed in the last section, they make us aware of the potential causal role of major factors such as culture, labor mobilization, institutional settings, and demographic and economic trends. Under many circumstances, the theories can be bridged in order to understand variations from one country or one policy area to another. But for the sake of clarity, it is better to look for a simpler explanation that relies on one theory. Yet, if this type of model fails to account for specific variations, we can start combining different approaches to fill the gaps in traditional, stand-alone social scientific theories like those reviewed in this chapter (Parsons 2007).

As for the debate on "American exceptionalism," none of these theories alone seems to explain what is unique about the United States in the domain of welfare state development. Instead of focusing on broad questions like the origins of "American exceptionalism," we may need to address more specific issues, such as explaining the historical and institutional differences between the fields of health care and old-age pensions, for example (Béland and Hacker 2004; Hacker 2002). Certainly, existing theories of welfare state development do provide insight into such key issues and, in the future, systematically combining these theories to tackle the unsolved mysteries of "American exceptionalism" would be useful. However, in the context of this short introduction to social policy, this is not possible and so we will instead turn our focus to more recent policy trends associated with the politics of retrenchment and restructuring.

4

Retrenchment and Restructuring

Social programs are expensive and, for most of your life, you are likely to help finance them though the various taxes you will pay. Of course, many of us know that, without social programs, millions of people could fall into poverty and face massive economic hardship that we find unacceptable. Moreover, we may feel that there is too much economic inequality and insecurity in our society, and that the state should do more, not less, to address these major problems. But as far as social policy is concerned, there is nothing free in this world, and we are increasingly aware of the fiscal trade-offs at the center of the welfare state. In fact, as shown in this chapter, concerns about the fiscal future of the welfare state have become widespread in recent decades. Before the 1973 oil crisis and the economic downturn it helped to create, the expansionary movement that had characterized much of the post-World War II era in the United States and other developed countries seemed unstoppable. Yet in less than a decade, the economic crisis, combined with related factors such as the rise of market liberalism, triggered a major transformation in the politics of social policy. In a new era of fiscal austerity, welfare state expansion no longer constituted the inescapable political and social horizon of the time, as it had during the 1950s and 1960s.

This chapter focuses on the contemporary welfare state politics, which is largely about retrenchment and restructuring. Starting with the widely debated work of Paul Pierson (1994, 2001), the nature of what he and others label the "new politics of the welfare state" is discussed; the scope of the changes that have affected social programs created before and during the post-war era is then assessed. The chapter is divided into three main sections. The first section examines the difference between the politics of expansion and the politics of retrenchment and restructuring. The second section takes a global look at the scope of social policy change that has taken place in developed societies, with a particular focus on the debate between proponents of path dependence, such as Pierson, and those who emphasize transnational convergence, such as Neil Gilbert (2002). The third section revisits the theories of welfare state development presented in Chapter 3 to assess their potential contribution to the retrenchment and restructuring debate.

The Retrenchment Debate

Changes in economic and political conditions in the 1970s led to a gradual decline of the post-war logic of welfare state expansion. In the aftermath of the 1973 oil crisis, deteriorating economic conditions as well as changing ideological and political circumstances called into question the Keynesian model of economic regulation that had promoted post-war welfare state expansion in the United States and most other developed countries. The main reason for the decline of Keynesianism was its perceived inability to reverse an unexpectedly prolonged economic downturn. Although several recessions marked the post-war era, the economic problems of the 1970s were deeper and more enduring, which weakened the foundation of the post-war economic and social order and the Keynesian, statist creed that had triumphed during the 1950s and especially the 1960s.[1] Commenting on the American economic situation during the 1970s, historian Edward Berkowitz has stressed the magnitude of the crisis, which was rooted in the backdrop of the post-war experience:

> After the great run of post-war prosperity, the state of the economy slid into stagflation for much of the period between 1973 and 1982.

This downturn differed from other post-war recessions that had featured business shutdowns and temporary layoffs. Although those things occurred in the seventies, they happened in a more sustained and deeper way and with the added twist of inflation accompanying the slowdowns. It looked at the time as though a crucial climacteric had been reached and that the great streak of economic growth that characterized the post-war period was over for good. (2006: 53)

That bleak economic context led a number of prominent economists and conservative think tanks to promote a return to market liberalism while attacking both Keynesianism and the idea of "big government."[2] Although economists such as Friedrich Hayek (2007) had long criticized the welfare state, the new economic context dramatically increased the interest in market liberalism among experts, business leaders, and politicians, and instead of remaining the seemingly "old-fashioned" approach it had been during most of the post-war era, it gained more ideological and political clout, starting in the late 1970s and early 1980s. Simultaneously, a growing number of businesses began subsidizing conservative think tanks in order to promote market liberalism and to reshape the image of private business, which had suffered tremendously during the previous decade (Edsall 1984). The expansion and multiplication of conservative think tanks such as the Heritage Foundation is directly related to this push to promote both market liberalism and business power (Rich 2004).

Simultaneously, in the United States, a social movement known as the "tax revolt" reacted against the removal of traditional tax privileges occurring through the modernization and standardization of state property taxes.[3] According to Isaac Martin (2008), many citizens were offended by the abolition of these traditional tax privileges, which had long protected them against market insecurity and instability. Even if it emerged as a diverse movement from an ideological standpoint, the state-level "tax revolt" culminated in 1978 with the adoption of the conservative Proposition 13, a ballot initiative that led to the creation of an enduring property tax limitation in the state of California. At the time, the victory of this conservative initiative was widely understood as a clear message to state and federal politicians. Soon after the enactment of Proposition 13 in California, similar tax limits were adopted in other states while alternatives to this conservative approach lost much ground. In Washington, well beyond the issue of property taxes, Republicans like presidential candidate and former California Governor Ronald Reagan moved massive tax cuts to the center of their agenda (Martin 2008).

Politically, at the international level, the 1979 election of the Conservative government of Margaret Thatcher in the United Kingdom became the symbol of this re-emergence of market liberalism in developed countries (see, e.g., Evans 2004; Letwin 1993). Known as the "Iron Lady," Thatcher confronted labor unions, privatized state-owned enterprises, and attacked the UK welfare state, which had expanded during the post-war era. Ideologically, the Thatcher government actively promoted personal responsibility and private ownership as the central component of a conservative, free-market reaction against statism. In a country where the state owned many enterprises and housing facilities, restoring the sacred and dominant nature of private property became a key ideological imperative. Explicitly inspired by the ideas of conservative economists such as Hayek, Thatcher's economic model became known as "popular capitalism" (Saunders and Harris 1994; Teles 1998). According to this vision, UK citizens needed greater opportunities to participate, as owners and investors, more actively in the development of UK capitalism. Conservative in nature, the popular capitalism discourse celebrated the economic and moral virtues of privatization and personal responsibility while denouncing welfare dependency and the "nanny state." Overall, Thatcherism aggressively promoted a coherent, free-market ideological campaign against the welfare state that legitimized cutbacks and privatizations (Schmidt 2002).

Less than two years after Thatcher became the UK prime minister, Ronald Reagan moved into the White House, where he articulated a similar market ideology centered on deregulation, tax cuts, and personal responsibility (see, e.g., Brownlee and Graham 2003; Kengor and Schweizer 2005). President Reagan's discourse on economic and social affairs, like that of Prime

Minister Thatcher (Hall and Jacques 1983), combined populism and market liberalism, which he turned against big government. This synthesis of populism and market liberalism is clearly evident in this famous excerpt from Reagan's Inaugural Address, in which he explicitly refers to the economic crisis of the 1970s:

> In this present crisis, government is not the solution to our problem; government is the problem. From time to time we've been tempted to believe that society has become too complex to be managed by self-rule, that government by an elite group is superior to government for, by, and of the people. Well, if no one among us is capable of governing himself, then who among us has the capacity to govern someone else? (Reagan 1981)

Essentially, Reagan pushed for massive tax cuts, as part of his pro-business stance, supported increases in military spending related to his aggressive anti-Soviet ideology, and defended traditional family values associated with the religious and cultural right. The core ideological and political base of this former Hollywood actor became known as the "Reagan coalition": the three major constituencies at the center of it were pro-business voters and proponents of market liberalism; anti-communists supporting a strong stance against the Soviet Union; and the religious right seeking to both fight secularism and restore traditional family values. In turn, these constituencies corresponded to the three main factions of the post-war conservative movement: libertarians, anti-communists, and traditionalists (Nash 1996).

As for social policy, both Thatcher and Reagan articulated a pro-market critique of the modern welfare state, which they depicted as a wasteful and overly bureaucratic machine that encouraged state dependency rather than self-reliance. To promote privatization and personal responsibility, they pushed for fiscal austerity and a reduction in social spending. To balance the budget and stimulate free trade, Thatcher and Reagan, each of whom was strongly supported by business groups and the wealthy, borrowed from conservative economic thinkers. Reagan also promoted a transformation of American federalism, in the sense of greater state autonomy (Conlan 1998). His push for decentralization represented yet another attempt to reduce the role of the federal government in American society and, more specifically, to reverse the trend that had triumphed during the New Deal and the post-war era: the expansion of the federal welfare state. Interestingly, the 1981 tax cuts, for which Reagan had pushed, helped stimulate the growth in federal deficits, which increased pressures on Congress to cut federal social programs in the name of fiscal responsibility (Pierson 1994).

Scholars have long debated the nature and long-term impact of the reforms enacted in the United Kingdom and the United States during the 1980s. Among these scholars, Paul Pierson is the most influential. In his 1994 book *Dismantling the Welfare State?*, he does more than analyze social policy reform under Thatcher and Reagan; he sketches a general theory of what he calls the "new politics of the welfare state." For Pierson, the Thatcher and Reagan years brought about the crystallization of a new political logic – retrenchment – that stands in sharp contrast to the post-war logic of expansion. Simply put, the concept of retrenchment refers to policy efforts aimed at curtailing social programs in a new economic and political context in which fiscal austerity is a major policy imperative.

In his book, Pierson establishes three major "ground rules" for the study of retrenchment. First, scholars studying the politics of retrenchment should examine both short-term and long-term spending cuts: "Governments interested in curtailing social programs may enact policies that cut spending immediately; they may also enact changes to be phased in over time, the full effects of which may not be felt for many years. . . . Benefit or eligibility restrictions may exempt current recipients, affecting only new beneficiaries" (p. 14). Pierson's observation is interesting because it points out that major cuts in benefits could take years or even decades to materialize, which complicates the analysis of spending patterns in an era of fiscal austerity. For example, in 1983, Congress agreed to increase Social Security's regular retirement age from sixty-five to sixty-seven between the years 2000 and 2022. The goal was to reduce the long-term costs of the program without affecting current and soon-to-become Social Security recipients, a situation that could have proved highly unpopular (Light 1995).

In his second ground rule, Pierson (1994) argues that the study of retrenchment should focus on both program structure and program spending (p. 14). Following the lead of Esping-Andersen (1990), he claims that raw spending figures do not necessarily tell the whole story about social programs and their development over time. For instance, spending data that are relatively stable over time could hide profound changes in the way funds are allocated. Program design, which is a critical aspect of the politics of retrenchment, is not only about cutting social spending but also about reallocating existing resources in order to pursue specific policy objectives. In the field of welfare reform, untouched benefit levels could conceal huge changes in eligibility criteria, such as the imposition of strict work obligations for able-bodied recipients. As Pierson puts it, "a study of welfare state change must focus on structure as well as size. To discuss retrenchment rather than cuts is to analyze political conflicts over the character of the welfare state" (p. 15). To return to the previous welfare example, even in the absence of spending cuts, the imposition of strict work requirements is a form of retrenchment since it promotes a social assistance model that departs from the dominant post-war logic of unconditional entitlements by making access to benefits conditional. Overall, it is a mistake to think that retrenchment is only about cuts in benefits and spending.

Pierson's third ground rule is that there are not one but two types of retrenchment: programmatic and systemic (pp. 15–17). As the term suggests, the concept of programmatic retrenchment is straightforward and only concerns direct changes to existing social programs: for example, when a program is revised or abolished in the name of fiscal control. Systematic retrenchment is a broader and potentially trickier concept, as it involves indirect changes to the economic and political landscapes, changes that may in fact promote direct program retrenchment over time: "Policy changes that alter the context for future spending decisions – what can be termed systemic retrenchment – may be as important as changes in spending or program structure 'within' the welfare state itself"

(p. 15). In short, to understand how retrenchment can take place over a longer period of time, students of social policy must keep the "big picture" in mind.

According to Pierson, policymakers typically employ four political tactics to alter the context of future policy decisions toward greater retrenchment. First, de-funding strategies, such as tax cuts, can be pursued to increase fiscal pressures that may facilitate programmatic retrenchment down the road. The tax cuts enacted at the beginning of the Reagan presidency correspond to this type of programmatic retrenchment. Coupled with major increases in military spending, these tax cuts resulted in serious budget deficits that helped to legitimize cuts in social programs and other forms of programmatic retrenchment. Second, policymakers supporting the retrenchment agenda can attempt to reduce existing popular support for the social programs they seek to curtail, or even abolish, by increasing the availability of alternative, private social benefits. Third, politicians can alter the "rules of the game," through changes in political institutions that could help them implement their retrenchment agenda (p. 16). For instance, retrenchment advocates may push for welfare state decentralization if they think it could lead to a "race to the bottom" that would reduce average benefit levels over time. Fourth, government officials can weaken the political clout of constituencies that traditionally oppose retrenchment: for example, in the form of attacks against the labor movement. Although such attacks are not directly aimed at the welfare state, they can reduce the influence of actors that would normally stand in the way of direct attempts at programmatic retrenchment.

These tactical examples point to the nature of retrenchment as a specific type of political activity that is distinct from the logic of the post-war welfare state expansion. In his 1994 work, Pierson draws extensively on the concepts of "credit claiming" (Mayhew 1974) and "blame avoidance" (Weaver 1986) to stress the contrast between the politics of expansion and the politics of retrenchment. Credit claiming concerns the competition that occurs between elected officials who want to receive political credit for new or expanded social benefits; blame avoidance refers to their attempts to protect themselves against any potential discontent that may stem from unpopular policy decisions associated with retrenchment.[4] According to Pierson, the shift from expansion to retrenchment that began in the mid- to late 1970s led to a decrease in the use of credit-claiming strategies and an increase in blame-avoidance strategies. This occurred because, if expansion is often popular, retrenchment is a risky political activity as constituencies are likely to punish the elected officials blamed for particular cutbacks and other unpopular decisions.

Pierson stressed the role of blame avoidance in the politics of retrenchment because he believes that during the post-war era, welfare state expansion created large social constituencies that have helped shield some large social programs against comprehensive retrenchment efforts: "With these massive programs have come dense interest-group networks and strong popular attachments to particular policies, which present considerable obstacles to reform" (1996: 146). The case of American Social Security offers an example of how constituencies are generated by the process of welfare state development (Campbell 2003).For instance, interest groups such as the American Association of Retired Persons (AARP) have emerged to form the well-organized and seemingly powerful "gray lobby" (Pratt 1993). According to Pierson (1996: 151), this type of constituency plays a much greater role today than traditional actors like labor unions, which were more central in the post-war era.[5] More generally, because retrenchment is a distinct political activity taking place in a different context than the politics of expansion, a new theoretical framework is necessary to understand how the politics of retrenchment work.

As a consequence, Pierson (1994) formulated such a framework, which centers on the concept of blame avoidance and the idea that social programs create constituencies and vested interests that complicate the actions of political actors pursuing various retrenchment strategies. Thus, his analytical framework draws explicitly on historical institutionalism, an approach that stresses the political weight of existing policy arrangements and the more general idea that "policy creates politics."

In *Dismantling the Welfare State?*, Pierson offers a comparative analysis of social policy reform in the United Kingdom and the United States during the 1980s. This analysis backs his general claims that retrenchment is a political logic distinct from expansion and that many of the policies adopted in earlier decades created powerful vested interests that complicated the Thatcher and Reagan administrations' efforts to downsize the welfare state in a fashion consistent with their free-market, anti-big-government agenda. Its starting point is the fact that Thatcher and, especially, Reagan failed to implement the most conservative aspects of their social policy agenda. In the case of Social Security, President Reagan faced so many attacks from Democrats and other supporters of this popular and well-entrenched program that, in order to tackle the fiscal crisis affecting it, he was forced to launch a moderate, bipartisan commission that favored the status quo rather than radical, pro-market reforms that could have transformed or even abolished Social Security (Light 1995). In the United Kingdom, Prime Minister Thatcher's effort to abolish the old-age insurance scheme (State Earnings Related Pension Scheme [SERPS]) adopted in the 1970s failed miserably, and she had to settle for a more modest, incremental reform (Pierson 1994).

Perhaps the only radical form of programmatic retrenchment that took place in Britain during the Thatcher years was in the field of public housing, where the capacity to sell existing public units to tenants at a discount made widespread policy privatization possible. When Margaret Thatcher and the Conservative Party came to power, the United Kingdom had a very large pool of public housing (Pierson 1994: 75–6), but less than two decades later, two housing experts commenting on the impact of Thatcher's housing policy reforms noted: "There has been a revolution in home ownership over the past twenty years. Groups of people who in the past might never have expected to own their own homes now do so" (Johnson and Tanner 1998: 368). Pierson (1994) depicts housing reform in Thatcher's Britain as an exception to the basic rule that social policy retrenchment and privatization are rarely successful in that politicians attempting to achieve path-departing reforms in well-established policy areas typically face the opposition of powerful constituencies.

Assessing Recent Changes

Many scholars have followed Pierson in emphasizing institutional inertia and path dependence (i.e., the idea that radical change is rare largely because of the vested interests that policies create over time). However, a growing body of literature offers alternative frameworks that can account for transformative processes that, it is argued, can reshape the social policy systems created before and during the post-war period (e.g., Béland and Waddan 2010a; Clasen and Siegel, 2007; Hacker 2004; Hinrichs and Kangas 2003; Streeck and Thelen 2005; Thelen 2004). A good way to draw attention to potential path-departing processes is to explore the role of incremental change in the welfare state.

One useful concept here is layering, which refers to "the grafting of new elements onto an otherwise stable institutional framework. Such amendments . . . can alter the overall trajectory of an institution's development" (Thelen 2004: 35).[6] An example of layering in contemporary American social policy is the expansion of personal savings accounts alongside Social Security (Hacker 2004). Additionally, according to Jacob Hacker (2004), the absence of reforms aimed at adapting existing policies to a changing social and economic context can alter their meaning and effects. This is what he calls "policy drift." In the United States, he notes, the contemporary reduction in many employment-based health and pension benefits is an example of "policy drift," as it is a major social policy transformation that is not primarily the result of legislative action, but the product of changing economic circumstances and the absence of reforms aimed at neutralizing their negative effects.

Focusing on this type of incremental change does not mean that institutional revision (i.e., systematic reforms) has become unimportant (Hacker 2004). Recent prominent cases of institutional revision in the United States include the 1996 welfare reform, the 1997 creation of SCHIP (State Children's Health Insurance Program), and the 2003 Medicare reform (Béland and Waddan 2010a; Howard 2006). Interestingly, the first reform is a dramatic example of retrenchment that resulted in the abolition of a large federal social program (AFDC). The two other reforms are prime examples of expansionary legislation that increased the federal government's role in health-care policy: SCHIP (now CHIP) covered millions of previously uninsured children, and the 2003 reform made prescription drug coverage part of the Medicare program. More so than SCHIP, and, partly because it profited the pharmaceutical industry so much, the Republican-sponsored 2003 Medicare reform favored a major increase in federal health spending. However, the reform also promoted market principles consistent with the conservative creed (Hacker and Pierson 2005; Jaenicke and Waddan 2006). Another interesting policy development taking place in the United States during the 1980s and 1990s was the expansion of the Earned Income Tax Credit (EITC) program: "When the EITC was first enacted in 1975, it was a modest benefit, but it was expanded considerably in 1986 and then again in 1990 and 1993. By 1996, nearly 20 million families were receiving EITC benefits, and annual federal outlays approached US$25 billion, almost double AFDC expenditures" (Quadagno and Street 2006: 307; see also Howard 2006; Myles and Pierson 1997). This is a prominent case of recent policy expansion in the American welfare state, and so is the 2010 health-care reform discussed in Chapter 5.

Overall, in the United States, although retrenchment is likely to remain on the agenda in some policy areas, welfare state expansion is a central feature of the contemporary social policy landscape, as EITC, SCHIP, the 2003 Medicare reform, and the 2010 health-care reform demonstrate. This situation is not unique to the United States. Since the 1980s, social programs in areas such as employment policy, family policy, and long-term care for the elderly have been created or expanded in many developed countries (Bonoli 2005). Retrenchment, welfare state expansion, and more subtle policy changes such as the incremental layering of new provisions within existing frameworks can also take place simultaneously in different policy areas. This occurred in the United States during the Clinton and the George W. Bush presidencies, during which debates on Social Security privatization and the expansion of the government's role in health-care were prominent (Béland and Waddan 2010a). In the end, as Jill Quadagno and Debra Street argue in their subtle assessment of the policy change that took place during both presidencies, contradictory tendencies are at play in contemporary welfare state reform:

> In the United States, programs that were constructed during the New Deal of the 1930s and the Great Society of the 1960s were revamped in various ways. At issue is whether these changes represent a major policy paradigm shift or merely a reshaping at the margins. Some evidence suggests that the United States is moving toward becoming an enabling state, at least in those programs that target the working-age population. The demise of AFDC and the expansion of the EITC promote work and target benefits. Less clear are recent directions in the social insurance programs that mainly serve the older population. Social Security has thus far remained immune to privatization proposals (although the options on the national political agenda have experienced a major transformation). Medicare has always incorporated the private sector into the administration of funds and the delivery of services, but recent policy measures have been designed to give the private insurance industry a much larger role. (2006: 212–13)

As suggested here, depending on the policy area and the specific program at stake, moving in several directions at once, the contemporary social policy landscape is much more complex than Pierson's theory would have us believe. This is true in the United States and in other developed countries as different as Canada (Rice and Prince 2000), France (Palier 2002), Japan (Shinkawa 2008), the Netherlands (Cox, 2001), and Sweden (Blyth, 2002).

These remarks suggest that the concept of retrenchment is too narrow to encompass all the significant changes in social policy that have taken place since the 1970s (Palier 2006). The concept of policy restructuring is a better alternative for attempting to make sense of broad contemporary trends, since it can encompass both retrenchment and other forms of policy change that may include welfare state expansion. The term "restructuring" is used widely in contemporary social policy research (see, e.g., Baker 2006; Timonen 2003), and it has the advantage of not reducing recent changes to what Pierson defines as retrenchment, which is just one aspect of social policy change in today's developed societies.

As a theoretical issue, restructuring is part of an ongoing debate in the recent social policy literature that centers on the questions: Since the 1970s, what has been the dominant pattern of policy change in developed welfare states? Have national welfare regimes followed the paths that crystallized before and during the post-war era, or have recent economic and political pressures reduced cross-national differences and brought about true convergence among developed nations? On one side of the debate, a number of scholars, following the lead of Pierson (1996), emphasize the weight of existing institutional arrangements and the related role of path dependence in contemporary social policy reform. These scholars reject the idea that some of the economic and political pressures mentioned earlier in this chapter have eroded the major institutional differences between countries that Esping-Andersen (1990) tried to account for in his welfare regime typology. Interestingly, Esping-Andersen (1996: 24) even coined an expression – "'frozen' welfare state landscape" – to describe what he understands as the inertia of contemporary welfare regimes. Although they refrain from talking about frozen landscapes, authors of recent books about contemporary social policy suggest that powerful institutional logics and vested interests have prevented massive cross-national convergence from taking place (e.g., Castles 2004; Huber and Stephens 2001; Pierson 2001; Swank 2002). Indeed, although spending figures do not tell the whole story, even a superficial look at the evolution of social expenditure in a number of developed countries seems to confirm the enduring nature of cross-national policy differences (see Table 4.1).

Neil Gilbert represents scholars on the other side of the debate, who question this more static view. In his book *Transformation of the Welfare State* (2002), Gilbert challenges Pierson's argument about path dependence and the related emphasis on enduring national differences, using a broad analysis of social policy reform in the United States and Western Europe during the 1980s and 1990s. According to Gilbert,

> the welfare states of advanced industrial nations are undergoing a major transformation. . . . [The] change is from policies framed by a universal approach to publicly delivered benefits designed to protect

Table 4.1 The evolution of public social expenditure in selected OECD countries as a percentage of GDP

Country	1980	1985	1990	1995	2000	2005
Canada	13.7	17.0	18.1	18.9	16.5	16.5
France	20.8	26.0	25.1	28.6	27.9	29.2
Germany	22.7	23.2	22.3	26.5	26.2	26.7
Italy	18.0	20.8	20.0	19.9	23.3	25.0
Japan	10.6	11.4	11.4	14.3	16.5	18.6
Sweden	27.1	29.4	30.2	32.1	28.5	29.4
UK	16.7	19.8	17.0	20.2	19.2	21.3
USA	13.1	13.1	13.4	15.3	14.5	15.9

Source: Adapted from Organization for Economic Co-operation and Development (OECD) online database: http://stats.oecd.org/index.aspx

labor against the vicissitudes of the market and firmly held as social rights to policies framed by a selective approach to private delivery of provisions designed to promote labor force participation and individual responsibility. (pp. 3–4)

Gilbert calls this new transnational policy model an "enabling state," and he locates his argument about the spread of this model across developed countries squarely on the convergence side of the contemporary social policy–restructuring debate. For Gilbert, the transnational convergence toward the enabling state is triggered by two main sets of forces: (1) the international diffusion of the pro-market ideas consistent with the enabling state model; and (2) the intensification of objective demographic, economic, and fiscal pressures related to factors such as population aging and capital mobility. According to him, the convergence brought about by these forces is not absolute, and the national-level political factors mean that, although the enabling state model is gaining ground in all developed countries, a number of significant cross-national differences remain. Gilbert uses a nautical metaphor to illustrate the complex relationship between growing convergence and residual cross national-differences in contemporary social policy:

Imagine the advanced industrial nations as ships of the welfare state, afloat on a large bay at ebb tide. As the tide recedes, they are all pulled in the same direction – converging toward the mouth of the bay. Moving in roughly the same direction, away from the shore, but not exactly toward the same final destination, some of the ships form small clusters that sail along on similar headings, whereas others chart independent courses. Thus, the modern welfare states expanded and branched off in various directions as they rode the ebb tide of economic development from the early 1960s to the late 1980s. But the tide has changed. When the 1990s came to a close, the ships of the welfare state were drawn back into the bay as a flood tide of new structural pressures and sociopolitical forces narrowed the channel of maneuverability and transformed the conventional arrangements for social welfare. (p. 22)

Gilbert's metaphor highlights the weight of transnational pressures that constrain social policy restructuring while pushing it in the direction of the pro-market enabling state.

In response to scholars such as Esping-Andersen (1996) and Duane Swank (2002), who reject the idea of major transnational convergence in policy design and outcomes, Gilbert (2002) argues that the true scope of a convergence produced by these factors is seldom obvious at first glance. Especially in countries where the welfare state is a major source of national pride, policymakers and welfare advocates tend to minimize the full extent of policy change occurring in their society. Recent scholarship on the discourse on social democracy in Sweden supports Gilbert's claim (Cox 2004). Quantitative analyses focusing on citizenship rights provide additional support for Gilbert's claim that major change has occurred since the 1980s and make it possible to talk about a transnational decline in social rights across the developed world (Korpi 2003).

Unfortunately, those on both sides of the policy change debate frequently fail to recognize that it is perhaps too early to draw definite conclusions about the direction of welfare state restructuring in contemporary societies. The time-frame is a crucial element when assessing the scope of possible welfare state convergence (Campbell 2004). Back in the late 1960s, few scholars predicted the shift from pure and simple expansion to retrenchment and restructuring that would take place less than a decade later. Today, it would be problematic to imagine that the trends identified by

Gilbert and others will go on for several more decades. If they do, however, convergence may well become an enduring reality and major differences between countries may keep declining over time, in the sense of the enabling state. Conversely, the tide Gilbert refers to may undergo a sudden change due to unexpected economic and/or political transformations that reduce the transnational pressures associated with the idea of welfare state convergence.

Because it can sometimes take decades to assess the enduring nature of particular social and economic trends, a careful approach to welfare state convergence and path dependence is required. As scholars debate the nature and meaning of recent welfare state changes, we need to recognize that the contemporary social policy landscape is characterized by both change and continuity, and that variations from one country to another and from one policy area to another within the same country remain significant. By keeping this basic point in mind, we can study the fate of particular nations and social programs within the context of the "big picture". However, when launching this type of empirical study, we need to have clear operational definitions of "convergence" and "path dependence"; otherwise, these concepts can become so vague that any reform can be described as corresponding to them in one way or another (Quadagno and Street 2006: 313).

Even when remaining neutral in the convergence–path dependence debate, it is possible to follow Gilbert (2002) by acknowledging a number of social policy trends that are present across the developed world. The best way to discuss these trends in relationship to the American situation is to review distinct policy areas. The goal is simply to draw on the work of Gilbert and others to map recent trends in welfare state restructuring in the United States and other developed countries, not to support or refute the convergence thesis. For the sake of conciseness, we will only look at two policy areas that were first discussed in Chapter 1: (1) work, unemployment, and welfare; and (2) pensions.

In the field of work, unemployment, and welfare, many countries have experienced a push toward what is known as "activation" (e.g., Cox 1998; Gilbert 2002: 61–3; Jenson and Saint-Martin 2006; Rosanvallon 2000). Proponents of activation believe that "passive" programs that provide income support to the unemployed should be reformed to include "active" provisions aimed at putting people back to work through training opportunities, work obligations, and even time limits, such as those imposed as part of the 1996 American welfare reform. Interestingly, the idea of activation is not always located on the right of the ideological spectrum, and actors from different political orientations have embraced it. In fact, activation as a social policy model originated in Scandinavia, where the quest for full employment has long been a dominant component of the social-democratic model. And, in recent decades, Denmark has adopted bold activation measures, according to which "welfare recipients who reject a fair offer of training, educational activities, and placement in jobs can have their benefits reduced by up to 20 percent" (Gilbert 2002: 63). In the United States, although the idea of workfare related to activation is found in conservative discourse on personal responsibility, "third-way" leader Bill Clinton ended up embracing a less punitive model of workfare during the 1992 presidential campaign.[7] However, this third-way vision was not part of the conservative welfare reform package that President Clinton signed four years later in order to advance his chances of reelection in 1996 (Béland, Vergniolle de Chantal, and Waddan 2002). In Canada, during the 1990s, cuts to unemployment insurance benefits and tighter eligibility criteria were combined with the development of new training programs for the unemployed (Campeau 2005; Hale 1998); at the provincial level, significant cutbacks in social assistance benefits further reduced the protection offered (Boychuk 2006). In the United Kingdom, third-way Labour Prime Minister Tony Blair made activation a priority after his 1997 election, a situation that resulted in a redefinition of the rights and obligations of the unemployed and the advent of conditional entitlements (Dwyer 2004). Across the English Channel, France began implementing mild activation policies in the late 1980s and early 1990s (Palier 2002; Rosanvallon 2000).

Overall, the activation policies of these countries have helped to redefine the relationship between social rights and citizenship obligations:

> Rather than viewing rights (consequently welfare entitlements) as absolute claims, there is an increasing tendency to view them as negotiated claims that balance not only the freedom and autonomy of the claimant, but also the concerns and voices of other members of society. Obligations can be pressed because taxpayers have a right to demand that governments be accountable for the money they spend. (Cox 1998: 12)

Although this general tendency is present across the developed world, cross-national differences in social rights for the unemployed remain significant because activation policies vary from one country to another – specifically, in the way in which the state uses both the "carrot" and the "stick" approaches (Gilbert 2002: 63). For instance, there is a major gap between the 1996 American welfare reform, where personal responsibility is emphasized over state responsibility, and the French model of social solidarity, where the responsibility of the state toward the unemployed remains much more central (Béland and Hansen 2000). So far, in the field of unemployment and welfare, the transnational diffusion of activation policies has yet to eliminate major institutional differences between countries. Only time will tell if, along the road, the global push for activation will lead to further institutional convergence.

In the field of pension policy, demographic pressures stemming from population aging and the economic push to promote personal savings have led a number of countries to reshape their public pension systems. This trend, although not as striking as the development of activation policies in the field of unemployment and welfare, is especially intriguing because, according to John Myles and Paul Pierson (2001), retirement policy is an area where path-dependent change is the norm, given that modern pension systems have created powerful constituencies and long-term commitments that, in most countries, represent strong obstacles to path-departing reform. Since the 1980s, however, a number of countries have transformed their public pension system in ways that challenge the path dependence thesis. Take Sweden, for example. In the mid-1990s, this social-democratic country adopted a comprehensive reform that refuted the idea that radical change is highly unlikely in the pension-policy domain (Anderson 2005: 94). In a context of economic downturn and demographic change that could drastically increase pension spending over time, members of the country's main political parties agreed to a reform aimed at reducing long-term pension costs, among other objectives. In the end, the adopted reform transformed the Swedish pension system by abandoning the defined-benefit logic and implementing personal savings accounts that diverted a small portion of the country's 18.5 percent payroll tax. Thus, although provisions were made to protect low-income workers, this new pension system was a considerable departure from the post-war era system, which featured generous, defined-benefit entitlements (Anderson 2005; Marier 2008). Other countries in which major path-departing changes have taken place in the field of pension reform include Italy and Japan, the latter a rapidly aging society facing demographic decline (Shinkawa 2008).

In many other developed countries, the state has stimulated an increase in voluntary savings accounts, alongside public benefits (e.g., Hacker 2004). The World Bank, in its report *Averting the Old Age Crisis* (1994), explicitly encouraged such attempts to increase the reliance on personal savings in retirement policy. But, as President George W. Bush's unsuccessful 2005 campaign for Social Security privatization illustrates (Béland and Waddan 2010a), direct efforts to reshape public pension systems can fail because of the obstacles Pierson (1994; Myles and Pierson 2001) identifies in his work. Simply put, because they create large constituencies and are grounded in long-term commitments spanning several generations, these systems are hard to reform. Still, as the Swedish example suggests, path-departing reforms are possible, even within mature pension systems and especially when demographic pressures encourage politicians to unite in order to impose unpopular reforms such as benefit cuts. In this context, taking stability for granted is probably unwise and politically naïve.

Revisiting Theories of Welfare State Development

Our discussion of work, unemployment, and welfare and of pension policy suggests that the politics of retrenchment and restructuring are characterized by cross-national trends that can lead to limited forms of convergence in specific policy areas. Yet, major differences between countries remain, and it is crucial to account for them. To do so, we will revisit the four theories of welfare state development discussed in the previous chapter. Although it is appropriate to follow Pierson (1994, 1996) in acknowledging the contrast between the new politics of the welfare state and the old politics these theories focus on, there is strong evidence that such theories remain useful in the era of retrenchment and restructuring (Myles and Quadagno 2002). Another look at the four theories of welfare state development – industrialism, the power resource approach, historical institutionalism, and the cultural and ideational perspective – will shed more light on the determinants of policy change in the era of retrenchment and restructuring; at the same time, the factors emphasized in these theories can improve our understanding of the forces that can halt or trigger transnational convergence. As in Chapter 3, we assume that these theories, and the factors they stress, may complement one another in the analysis of policy change.

The emphasis on the economic and demographic forces central to industrialism, our first theory of welfare state development, remains relevant to the analysis of the politics of retrenchment and restructuring. As John Myles and Jill Quadagno claim:

> At the very moment when political theories of the welfare state seem to have relegated the "logic of industrialism" thesis with its emphasis on the overdetermining role of large impersonal economic forces to the critical list, the theory was revived in new form. Economic globalization and postindustrialism (along with its demographic correlates) are the new forces thought to be reshaping welfare states. (2002: 41)

For proponents of this economic and demographic perspective on retrenchment and restructuring, demographic aging and/or impersonal market forces such as financial globalization create overwhelming pressures on existing social policy arrangements that facilitate an international "race to the bottom" in terms of social protection (Mishra 1999). A clear presence in the work of Gilbert (2002) and others, this convergence-under-pressure vision contrasts with the institutionalist perspective put forward in Pierson's *Dismantling the Welfare State?* (1994).

But recognizing the key role of changing demographic and/ or economic forces does not necessarily lead to a negation of cross-national differences. In fact, variations in demographic and economic pressures can help account for at least some of these differences in the era of retrenchment and restructuring (Myles and Quadagno 2002). This is why those studying policy change in contemporary welfare states must pay close attention to economic and demographic factors, particularly financial globalization and demographic aging, and it is precisely why the final chapter devotes so much space to these two issues as part of a broader discussion on the future of social policy.

The focus on labor mobilization that is at the center of our second theory of welfare state development – the power resource perspective – is particularly insightful when dealing with countries where both labor unions and labor parties play a prominent role in policymaking.[8] This view challenges Pierson's (1996) bold claim about the declining role of labor in welfare state politics in the era of retrenchment. For Pierson, the labor movement is no longer a crucial actor in welfare state politics, partly because beneficiaries and organizations representing them like the AARP (American Association of Retired Persons) tend to replace labor unions and parties as the most powerful defenders of the welfare state. The American situation seems to confirm Pierson's argument. For example, between 1975 and 1991, the union density ratio dropped from nearly 29 percent to about 16 percent, a situation that directly contributed to a decline in labor's political influence (Galenson 1996: 2–3). The lack of a major, stand-alone labor party in the United States (Maioni 1998) exacerbated this situation.

From an international perspective, though, it is a mistake to assume that labor is much less central than before in welfare state politics. In France, for example, massive labor protests related to social policy issues are common. Although they do not always succeed in their efforts to fight retrenchment attempts, these large street protests, which can involve several million people from across the country, have forced French officials to amend or even change some of their reform proposals (Béland and Marier 2006; Bonoli 2000; Palier 2002). As for labor parties, there is strong quantitative evidence that their presence in government can affect policy outcomes (Huber and Stephens 2001), which, in turn, supports the idea that, in many countries, class mobilization remains a key aspect of the politics of retrenchment and restructuring. But, to understand the political influence of these parties, scholars must examine the nature of national party systems, as well as electoral systems. In short, to understand the role of class politics in the contemporary politics of social policy, it is useful to combine insights from both the historical institutionalism and the power resource perspectives (Huber and Stephens 2001).

As a supplement to the analysis of class politics, scholars Evelyne Huber and John Stephens (2001) have shown that the power resource approach can be extended to the issues of gender and, more specifically, women's political mobilization. Indeed, because policy outcomes are gendered, gender and women's mobilization should be key aspects of the scholarship on welfare state retrenchment and restructuring (Bashevkin 2000). In the context of economic and demographic pressures, a gendered analysis of retrenchment and restructuring is potentially compatible with insight from historical institutionalism (i.e., policy legacies reflecting patterns of gender inequality can impact political debates on social policy). Overall, because group mobilization remains dominant in the politics of contemporary social policy, it is not appropriate to discard the power resource perspective altogether. Revising this approach to account for both gendered relations and the enduring weight of political institutions and policy legacies is probably the best way to keep it relevant in contemporary debates about retrenchment and restructuring.

Our third theory of welfare state development, historical institutionalism, is probably the most debated perspective in terms of the politics of retrenchment and restructuring, partly because Pierson (1994) draws explicitly from it. Although institutionalist scholars recognize the role of the economic and demographic pressures noted above, they believe that existing national institutions and

115

policy legacies mediate their impact on the welfare state (Weaver 2003). Indeed, these institutions and legacies can account for major cross-national differences and for variations from one policy area to another within the same country. For instance, institutionalist scholars argue that institutional factors like the characteristics of each national pension system can both moderate the impact of economic and demographic factors like population aging and explain enduring cross-national differences in pension policy (Béland and Shinkawa 2007). In this context, comparisons between programs within the same policy area are especially appropriate, as they help to assess the potential role of policy legacies and vested interests in more detail. For example, in the field of social assistance, the EITC (Earned Income Tax Credit) program is more robust politically than the now defunct AFDC (Aid to Families with Dependent Children) program because it protects the working poor, who tend to form a more active political constituency than the jobless single parents who typically collect welfare benefits. However, the analysis of policy feedback from existing programs should also include a discussion of the deeply entrenched cultural categories that embody the contrast between these programs and the constituencies stemming from them (Steensland 2007). This example shows that, as in the case of welfare state development, explanatory factors may be combined in order to account for major aspects of the politics of retrenchment and restructuring in contemporary societies.

The cultural and ideational perspective, our fourth theory of welfare state development, has some interesting things to say about the politics of retrenchment and restructuring. First, this perspective can shed light on trends that may promote transnational convergence; in particular, the literature on paradigms and policy diffusion can explain the transnational propagation of policy ideas that end up guiding the decision-making process in various countries. For instance, in the 1980s, fiscal austerity gained ground in Sweden largely because prominent economists there embraced neo-liberal (i.e., conservative) economic ideas similar to those of their counterparts in the United States and other developed countries. Evidence suggests that their embrace of neo-liberal ideas did not occur as an automatic reaction to new economic conditions but as a concerted attempt to master uncertainty and develop politically successful policy ideas in a changing environment (Blyth 2002). Another example of transnational diffusion is the adoption of workfare in the United Kingdom. First developed in the United States, this concept became influential in the United Kingdom during the Clinton years, after Tony Blair borrowed from Clinton's "third-way" vision to promote activation in social assistance policy (Daguerre 2004; King and Wickham-Jones 1999).

A second use of the cultural and ideational perspective, in the context of retrenchment and restructuring, has been to attempt to explain major cross-national differences in policy outcomes (e.g., Bhatia and Coleman 2003; Cox 2001; Pfau-Effinger 2005; Schmidt 2002). Although some of this work focuses on deeply rooted cultural differences between countries that may explain why policy convergence does not take place (Pfau-Effinger 2005), this type of scholarship is largely about how political discourse can explain transnational social policy differences (e.g., why a specific reform proposed in a number of countries fails in some of them but is adopted in others). A good example of this type of scholarship is the work of Robert H. Cox (2001), which considers why Denmark and the Netherlands, but not Germany, implemented comprehensive welfare reform in the 1990s. For this scholar, governing German politicians, as opposed to their Danish and Dutch colleagues, did not adequately construct the need to restructure welfare programs, which explains why their reform proposals went nowhere. What this type of scholarship suggests is that elected officials can create compelling political imperatives aimed at convincing citizens and key interest groups that reforms are necessary. In other words, in order to enact potentially unpopular measures, politicians generally need to convince other actors that the measures are both necessary and legitimate. In American society implicit references to racial prejudice and stereotypes are present in the political discourse surrounding policy issues like welfare reform, where race has long been a central issue (Schram, Soss, and Fording 2003). This attention to ideas and discourse does not mean that scholars should

117

ignore other, non-ideational factors such as demographic aging or political institutions, since such factors can interact with ideas and discourse to bring about welfare state change (e.g., Béland 2010; Campbell 2002; Hansen and King 2001; Padamsee 2009; Schmidt 2010; Walsh 2000).

Overall, these four theories of welfare state development offer stimulating insight into the politics of retrenchment and restructuring. Even if Pierson (1994) correctly stresses the peculiar nature of the "new politics of the welfare state" compared to those of the post-war expansion, discarding theoretical approaches that help account for policy change during that earlier period is simply a bad idea (Myles and Quadagno 2002). As suggested earlier, the causal factors put forward by these four approaches remain central to the current debate on policy change. The challenge faced by future researchers is to clearly distinguish between potential causal factors before conducting comparative studies about policy change in contemporary welfare states (Parsons 2007; for a different perspective on this issue, see Padamsee 2009). Finally, this type of analysis should take into account both legislative revisions and incremental forms of policy change (Hacker 2004; Thelen 2004).

Conclusion

This chapter has surveyed the current debate on policy change in contemporary welfare states, which owes a great deal to the work of Pierson and his many critics. Although Pierson is correct to assert that retrenchment operates according to a different political logic than the post-war politics of expansion, focusing exclusively on retrenchment is potentially misleading for two reasons. First, incremental changes in private benefits and socioeconomic conditions can result in substantive policy change in the absence of major legislative action (Hacker 2004). Second, beyond the issue of incremental change and private benefits, the "new politics of the welfare state" are not just about fiscal austerity and policy retrenchment, because, in recent decades, major new programs have been enacted while others have been expanded. Thus, the idea of retrenchment only partially captures the nature of the political logic that characterizes our era (Palier 2006). Furthermore, the four theories of welfare state development we have discussed remain most useful for contemporary social policy analysis, in part because they help us map the potential causal factors at play in the welfare state's new politics.

As for the debate on path dependence and transnational convergence, we must keep in mind that there is relatively little consensus on the global scope of the changes that have occurred since the mid-1970s. On one hand, in specific policy areas such as social assistance and pension reform, it is not hard to find powerful global trends such as the push for activation or the attempt to increase the reliance of citizens on personal retirement savings. A close look at other policy areas like health-care and family benefits would probably lead to the same basic conclusion about the existence of significant cross-national trends. For example, as evidenced in the next chapter, in the field of health-care reform, controlling the increase in medical costs has become a key policy imperative in many developed countries, including the United States. Regarding family benefits, they increasingly focus on supporting working parents in societies characterized by changing gender roles and labor market conditions (Bonoli 2005). On the other hand, although many of the pressures for change, such as demographic aging and changing gender roles, are present across the developed world, their pace of development and the ideological, institutional, and political factors that mediate their political impact on the welfare state can vary greatly from one country to another, which in turn limits the scope of policy convergence. At the transnational level, only time will tell if such broad demographic and economic pressures translate into an enduring form of policy convergence among developed nations. By focusing on some of the most significant demographic, economic, and social trends of our time, the next chapter gives us a better idea of what may await contemporary welfare states in the decades to come.

5

Looming Challenges

Many of us tend to see our long-term future, both individual and collective, as largely uncertain. Facing so much uncertainty, we may fear that the social programs we have today could become unsustainable or irrelevant. In this context, why should we care? Ironically, we should care precisely because our social and economic future seems so uncertain, and because improving our social programs could help us live a more secure life and perhaps spend more time with our family and friends instead of struggling to merely survive. As suggested in this book, the welfare state can impact many aspects of our lives, which is a good reason to think about its future. Although there is no consensus about how to improve social programs, we need to think hard about the challenges we face, and the reform opportunities stemming from them. Partly because most of us will pay for it for the rest of our lives and partly because social policy is about core issues like citizenship, responsibility, and solidarity, the welfare state is a key part of our individual and collective future. In other words, we cannot afford not to care.

Today, developed countries face significant social policy challenges, ranging from population aging and growing health-care costs to enduring inequalities and changing patterns of economic insecurity. In the case of the United States, the fragmented and limited scope of the American welfare state makes its situation particularly alarming, at least in terms of economic inequality and social insecurity. This is even truer in the aftermath of the

2008 financial crisis and the related recession, which hit millions of Americans especially hard. From foreclosures to rising unemployment rates, the recession illustrated the devastating scope of economic insecurity in one of the richest societies on earth.

The objective of this chapter is not to offer detailed forecasts about the fate of American and international social policy in the next few decades. As the impact of the Great Depression suggests, sudden economic change can have a direct impact not only on specific programs but also on welfare state politics at large. Moreover, alongside and frequently in conjunction with major economic shifts, unforeseen political episodes can steer the course of welfare state development. For instance, few people in the early 1970s predicted that, a decade later, conservative leaders would rule in both the United Kingdom and the United States and be pushing a neo-liberal agenda centered on deregulation, privatization, and tax cuts. In fact, in his 1973 book *The Coming of the Post-Industrial Society*, American sociologist Daniel Bell famously – and wrongly – predicted that national states would become increasingly involved in planning and regulating the economic and social order and neglected to consider the possibility of a conservative attack against the welfare state, which materialized just six years later with the election of the Thatcher government in Britain.[1]

This chapter then, to quote the subtitle of Bell's book, is not "A Venture in Social Forecasting" but a much more modest discussion of a number of issues that are present in contemporary debates on the future of social policy. Specifically, the chapter first turns to ongoing demographic, economic, and social transformations and highlight changing forms of inequality and insecurity in developed societies. As argued, newer challenges coexist with older, enduring problems such as income inequality and unemployment. The chapter then moves on to explore the relationship between globalization and social policy, which is often raised in contemporary debates on the future of the welfare state, both in the United States and elsewhere. After suggesting that national states remain the most central sources of social protection in developed countries, we look at the growing scholarship on the impact of globalization on social policy. Because this literature is so large, we can only focus on a limited number of issues, namely global inequalities, immigration, trade liberalization, foreign aid and the role of international organizations and transnational networks in the diffusion of policy ideas and "foreign models." Overall, this chapter shows that paying attention to these global forces as well as to issues like health-care costs and rising social inequalities is an excellent way to map the complex challenges facing contemporary welfare states, including the American one. As argued, many of these challenges have deep *political* implications that students of social policy should keep in mind.

Social, Demographic, and Economic Challenges

The debate on industrialism and the three other theories of welfare state development reminds us that modern social programs emerged largely as explicit responses to new social, demographic, and economic trends that stemmed from industrialization and urbanization. As previously discussed, in the United States, concerns about the negative consequences of industrialization and urbanization on the economic security of workers and their families became key political issues during the Progressive Era. At that time, following their European counterparts, American social reformers wrote entire books devoted to the analysis of new forms of social and economic insecurity and their ties to industrialization and urbanization. For these reformers, the social and economic risks of the industrial era differed from those associated with the agrarian era (mainly rural societies of the past), and these changing realities created a new risk structure that justified the enactment of innovative policies inspired by recent European reforms (e.g., Rubinow 1913; Seager 1910).

A century later, a new wave of academics, policy experts, and public intellectuals are learning from the current changing economic and social circumstances in order to design social policies adapted to our times. Never totally distinct from political debates on the future of the welfare state, the emerging literature is as diverse as the economic and social challenges we face today. For example, a recent growing component of this international scholarship is devoted to so-called "new social risks" (e.g., Armingeon and Bonoli 2006; Bonoli 2005; Esping-Andersen 1999; Esping-Andersen et al. 2002; Hacker 2006; Huber and Stephens 2006; Jenson 2004; Taylor-Gooby 2004). At the most general level, these new risks refer to

> situations in which individuals experience welfare losses and which have arisen as a result of the socio-economic transformations that have taken place over the past three to four decades and are generally subsumed under the heading of post-industrialisation. Above all, deindustrialisation and the tertiarisation of employment, as well as the massive entry of women into the labour force, have increased the instability of family structures and the destandardisation of employment. (Bonoli 2006: 5–6)

Thus, new social risks are related to the shift from an industrial to a postindustrial society, where the tertiary (i.e., service) sector is increasingly central to the economy. Although industrial work remains a primary source of employment in today's developed societies, the service sector has expanded dramatically over the last four decades, and this shift is a significant aspect of contemporary social policy.

Key factors associated with new social risks include changing family patterns, shifts in labor-market conditions, and the increasing demographic weight of the elderly population. These factors are at the root of social risks that range from single parenthood and having to care for sick relatives to possessing obsolete technical skills and lacking adequate social policy coverage because of one's precarious employment status (Bonoli 2005: 422–5). Although these social risks have long existed, the demographic and economic factors noted here make them more central today than they were during the post-World War II era, for example. At the same time, it is fair to say that these social risks have not displaced more traditional sources of inequality and insecurity like unemployment, which remains a prominent policy issue in developed societies (Jenson 2004). Consequently, we face older and newer challenges that may require major state actions to improve existing programs and create new policies capable of adapting modern welfare states to changing social, demographic, and economic circumstances.

Changing Labor Markets and Rising Economic Insecurity

Since the post-war era, developed countries have undergone economic transformations that have aggravated concrete forms of economic insecurity. The declining economic status of low-skilled workers is one of the most engrossing trends of our time. Giuliano Bonoli (2005) offers an excellent description of the decline in the economic status of these workers, experienced during the shift from an industrial to a postindustrial order:

> Low-skilled individuals have obviously always existed. However, during the postwar years, low-skilled workers were predominantly employed in the manufacturing industry. They were able to benefit from productivity increases due to technological advances, so that their wages rose together with those of the rest of the population. The strong mobilising capacity of the trade unions among industrial workers further sustained their wages, which came to constitute the guarantee of a poverty-free existence. Today, low-skilled individuals are mostly employed in the low value-added service sector or unemployed. Low value-added services such as retail sales, cleaning, catering and so forth are known for providing very little scope for productivity increases. . . . In countries where wage determination is essentially based on market mechanisms, this means that low-skilled individuals are seriously exposed to the risk of being paid a poverty wage ([Canada], US, UK, Switzerland). (p. 434)

Although it is possible to argue that some of these economic trends are tied to globalization, Bonoli is suggesting they acquire a different meaning from one country to another. The following discussion, which focuses on the United States, does not address the root causes of these trends. Instead, it simply explores their negative impact on economic security.

In the United States, the decline of the labor movement since the

1960s and the related weakening of employer-sponsored health and pension benefits have aggravated the challenges facing low-skilled workers. After World War II, many low-skilled workers could find well-paid, unionized jobs in the auto and steel industries, for example, and from the 1950s on, many of these jobs were tied to comprehensive health and pension coverage. Today, with the decline of many traditional industries, low-skilled workers are more likely to find a job at places like Wal-Mart and McDonald's, service-sector employers that offer low wages and limited social benefits while typically fighting unionization attempts (Dicker 2005). Many of these workers have little choice but to work part-time and/or during evenings and weekends, a situation that may compromise their family life. For women, lower wages can be insufficient to cover day-care expenses, especially when employers do not provide access to affordable child-care. Moreover, the fate of low-skilled American workers is related to racial and ethnic inequalities – African Americans and Hispanics are over-represented among low-skilled workers, a reflection of historically embedded forms of economic and social stratifiers. The availability of illegal, low-skilled immigrants and the increasing focus of American immigration policy on family reunification rather than on immigrant labor skills have aggravated this problem (Borjas 2006: 59).

Beyond the deteriorating status of low-skilled workers, a series of factors have weakened the economic security of many American citizens. Even before the onset of the 2008 recession, numerous signs of growing economic insecurity were apparent. For Jacob Hacker (2006), the most alarming symptom of this growing insecurity was the income instability affecting families:

American family incomes are now on a frightening roller coaster, rising and falling much more sharply from year to year than they did thirty years ago. Indeed, the *instability* of American families' incomes has risen substantially faster than the *inequality* of families' incomes. In other words, while the gaps between the rungs of the ladder of the American economy have increased, what has increased even more quickly is how far people slip down the ladder when they lose their financial footing. (p. 14)

Afraid of losing their jobs and the social benefits tied to them, millions of middle-class citizens must cope with increasing economic insecurity, which is no longer confined to immigrants, low-skilled workers, and other traditionally vulnerable segments of the population. Economic insecurity also has a major psychological component in that these millions of Americans spend a great deal of time worrying about their economic future and the fate of their loved ones. And, as Hacker notes, income instability data suggest that Americans "have good reason to think [they are insecure]" (p. 20), since they are facing a greater risk of sudden income loss than in the past. Although other factors such as rising divorce rates and changing family patterns have contributed to this problem, much of it stems from the changing nature of the American employment contract. Now, instead of focusing on the "shared fate" of workers and their employers as the old contract did, the new employment contract focuses on "individual gain" and "personal responsibility." In this new world, where labor unions are weaker than during the post-war years, accountability and performance take precedence over job security and the mutual, long-term commitment of both workers and employers. This new vision of the employment contract has intensified employment instability and, as a consequence, economic insecurity (pp. 66–7).

Gender and Family–Work Balance

The shift in family relations is another key social policy issue of our time. In recent decades, family relations have changed at an accelerated pace. One prominent feature of this transformation is the rise in divorce rates, which, in itself, is not a new phenomenon: "For example, in the United States from 1870 to 1980 the divorce rate multiplied by 13, going from 1.6 to 21.9 divorces [a year] per 1,000 married women. . . . These trends are similar for all Western nations permitting divorce" (Wilensky 2002: 8). Between 1980 and 2000, American divorce rates declined slightly but remained high from a long-term historical perspective. In general, higher divorce rates create major challenges in terms of child support, for example (Johnson and O'Brien-Strain 2000). Moreover, such divorce rates and the substantial number of single parents (despite the recent decline in teen pregnancies) increase the likelihood that these parents occupy a permanent and central place in the contemporary social landscape. The economic status of single parents is a major policy concern, in part because single mothers, who form the majority of this social category, are far more likely than the average population to be poor and/or jobless; in fact, fewer than half of American single mothers work full-time (Rodgers 2006: 49). Historically, the status of single mothers is tied to the welfare debate but, today, access to affordable child-care and training opportunities must be addressed if more single parents are to find better jobs and escape poverty. Dealing with these problems is one of the best ways to fight child poverty, as poor children are typically overrepresented in families headed by a single mother.

But contemporary social policy challenges related to changing family relations are not only about divorce and the fate of single parents, especially single mothers. This is true partly because all categories of women, including married ones, are increasingly participating in the labor market. Since World War II, the number of women working full-time has significantly increased across the developed world. In the United States, for example, female labor-force participation increased from 42 percent to 60 percent between 1973 and 1997 (Massey 2007: 46). Factors accounting for this trend include "the increase in schooling, delayed child-bearing and smaller families, and changes in marriage patterns. But lifetime work experience has increased among women of all educational and family statuses, suggesting that a pervasive behavioral shift has occurred among recent cohorts of women" (Bianchi 1995: 118). The result of this situation is rising numbers of dual-earner families. For instance, between 1960 and the late 1980s, "dual-earner families grew from under 25 percent to nearly 40 percent of all families, while families headed by single mothers increased from about 9 percent to around 23 percent" (McLanahan and Casper 1995: 16). In the mid-1990s, 93 percent of fathers and 69 percent of mothers aged between twenty-five and fifty worked full-time or part-time (Gornick and Meyers 2003: 59). Thus, in terms of the labor participation of mothers, the United States is on par with Canada and ahead of many countries belonging to the conservative welfare regime, such as Germany, Luxemburg, and the Netherlands, but far behind social-democratic Sweden, where 85 percent of women aged twenty-five to fifty worked full-time or part-time in the mid-1990s (Gornick and Meyers 2003: 59).

From a social policy perspective, the increase in dual-earner families is a substantial challenge when family–work balance is considered. Bonoli (2005) summarizes why the lack of balance between work and family life is a major social challenge, especially for women:

> The massive entry of women into the labour market has meant that the standard division of labour within families that was typical of the [post-war era] has collapsed. The domestic and child care work that used to be performed on an unpaid basis by housewives now needs to be externalised. It can be either obtained from the state or bought on the market. The difficulties faced by families in this respect (but most significantly by women) are a major source of frustration and can result in important losses of welfare, for example, if a parent reduces working hours because of the unavailability of adequate child care facilities. (p. 433)

Besides new child-care demands, the growing involvement of mothers in the formal labor market has created the need for better, more extensive maternal leaves. At the same time, given the slow transformation of parental roles related to changing gender relations and mothers' expanding participation in the labor market, fathers are increasingly called upon to play a greater role in child-rearing. Thus, more comprehensive *parental* leaves – not just maternal leaves – are needed. In the domain of paid parental leaves, because the United States lags behind Canada and many Western European countries (Gornick and Meyers 2003: 40), better paid-leave programs should be created to reduce the potential social risk of a serious imbalance between Americans' work and family lives. In addition to the issue of better parental leaves, the need for a more equal division of unpaid domestic labor between working mothers and fathers is widely debated in contemporary societies. For mothers who work full-time, performing most of the traditional housekeeping and child-rearing tasks on top of their labor-market obligations is frequently a major source of fatigue and stress, which could push them to work part-time and/or abandon their socially legitimate career ambition: "Although men have increased their hours of domestic works in recent decades, the increase has been far too modest to close the substantial gender gap in unpaid [domestic] work" (Gornick and Meyers 2003: 34). Finally, to return to the status of single parents, they face even more obstacles than married couples in terms of family–work balance (Bonoli 2005: 434). Overall, considering contemporary demographic and social trends, the need to help parents balance their family and work lives is a crucial element of current social policy debates and is likely to remain on the policy agenda for years and decades to come in the United States and elsewhere.

Demographic Aging and Population Change

Demographic aging is anything but a new phenomenon and, in the United States and other developed societies, factors such as higher life expectancies explain why the percentage of elderly people (those sixty-five years and older) has long been increasing (Congressional Budget Office 2005). Throughout the twentieth century in the United States, this percentage progressively increased from barely 4 percent to more than 12 percent. Over the next few decades, this trend should continue, with the proportion of Americans aged sixty-five years and older expected to reach 21 percent by 2050. It is worth noting that countries like Germany, Italy, and Japan face a much greater demographic challenge than the United States, which has significantly higher fertility rates – and a younger current and projected population – than these other developed countries (Gavrilov and Heuveline 2003). However, this remark does not negate the basic reality that, in the decades to come, demographic aging should have concrete consequences for the welfare state.

As far as the welfare state is concerned, demographic aging is significant for at least two major reasons. First, it can increase the number of those having to care for a frail (perhaps disabled but more typically elderly) relative with insufficient pension benefits, which is widely recognized as an increasingly pressing challenge in contemporary societies (Bonoli 2005: 434–5). The growing number of dependent and frail elderly persons is also likely to both increase health-care costs and create significant pressures on existing long-term-care facilities. In turn, the need for more comprehensive long-term-care facilities is related to changes in family trends and patterns of labor-market participation that make it more difficult for adult children, especially women, to care for their elderly parents on a full-time basis: "Smaller families and higher employment rates mean that the time and labour that was available in the home to provide care to relatives is no longer as readily available and it is certainly not 'costless'" (Jenson 2004: 16). Although many men care for elderly relatives, women are more likely to alter their career choices and make economic sacrifices to fulfill their care duties. As Jane Jenson (2004) notes in reference to the Canadian case, "while there are only very small gender differences in overall rates of caring for a person over 65, measures of consequences of caring, especially in employment, are gendered. Among women caring for a person over 65 and themselves aged 54–65, 17 percent reduced their work patterns, but only 11 percent of men in the same situation did the same" (p. 16). Interestingly, because greater female labor-market participation can help generate more funding for programs such as Medicare and Social Security, the fact that a growing number of women might feel obliged to leave the labor market to take care of an elderly parent is a key source of concern, not only in terms of gender equality but in terms of long-term funding issues. In addition to the need for better, more accessible long-term-care facilities and a more equal division of care for elderly relatives between women and men, more flexible work schedules could help adult children care for their elderly parents and preserve fulfilling careers. Overall, this idea of a more flexible work life could improve the family–work balance.

From a social policy perspective, a second major reason why demographic aging is significant is that the growing number and portion of elderly citizens in developed societies is already increasing the fiscal pressure on public and private pension schemes. In the long run, recent and future cuts in pension benefits aimed at reducing these fiscal pressures could negatively impact the future well-being of the elderly. Because the post-war expansion of public pension systems contributed to the reduction of poverty among the elderly, it is undeniable that direct or even indirect benefit cuts, such as an increase in the retirement age, could aggravate the situation. Part-time and low-skilled workers who have more limited access to private pensions and personal retirement savings than better-off workers would be especially at risk. Because elderly people constitute a growing segment of the population, higher rates of elderly poverty could affect millions of people. Indeed, compared to other developed countries like Canada, Germany, and Sweden, the United States is already witnessing higher rates of elderly poverty.[2] Thus, potential cuts in Social Security benefits could aggravate this problem, a problem that the United States has failed to adequately tackle, despite the post-war expansion of Social Security. In part due to their greater rates of electoral participation, elderly Americans make up a political constituency that is in a strong position to fight potential cutbacks that could make future retirees even more vulnerable to poverty than current retirees (Campbell 2003). At the same time, changing labor-market conditions and the related decline of defined-benefit private pensions (Ghilarducci 2008; Hacker 2004) mean the economic security of many future elderly citizens is at risk.

The focus of the contemporary American debate on the future of social programs for the elderly, such as Medicare and Social Security, is particularly interesting: there is much less political talk about poverty rates among the elderly and much more talk about the increasing number of beneficiaries related to population aging. The fear is that these programs could soon eat up enormous amounts of fiscal resources, which would crush the federal government and leave little room for other spending priorities, such as education. This is the "time bomb" scenario, which is centered on a pessimistic view of population aging and its impact on the welfare state (Altman 2005; Baker and Weisbrot 1999; Béland and

131

Waddan 2000). Clearly, this view is simplistic; as noted earlier, the United States is in a better situation than other developed countries to meet the challenge stemming from population aging (Béland 2005), which is not as dramatic as is commonly argued (Castles 2004). Although Medicare deserves serious attention due to the issue of rising health-care costs discussed below, Social Security could survive in the decades to come without dramatic adjustments such as massive, across-the-board benefit cuts (e.g., Aaron and Reischauer, 2001; Ghilarducci 2008; White 2001). Overall, in the United States as in other developed countries, there is no evidence that demographic aging is crushing the welfare state (Castles 2004). Although we face a significant demographic challenge, there is little basis for panic.

Health-Care Coverage and Spending

The future of health-care is a major issue in most developed welfare states, which struggle to control costs and maintain access to care. In the United States, this issue is particularly crucial. For example, with the current increase in medical costs, those without health insurance face the prospect of unbearable personal debt if they ever need a long hospital stay. In fact, "high medical debt is the leading cause of personal bankruptcy, the most common reason people lose their homes or cannot get a mortgage or rental property, and makes them unwilling to seek additional health services" (Hunt and Knickman 2008: 71; for an overview, see Seifert 2005). As the *New York Times* reported in late 2008, during a recession that exacerbated both health and economic insecurity: "As increasing numbers of the unemployed and uninsured turn to the nation's emergency rooms as a medical last resort, doctors warn that the centers – many already overburdened – could have even more trouble handling the heart attacks, broken bones and other traumas that define their core mission" (Abelson 2008). Although the 2008 recession made things worse, overcrowded emergency rooms are one of the negative consequences of having so many people living without health insurance coverage, a situation that the 2010 reform discussed below seeks to address.

Overall, the lack of insurance coverage results in social insecurity, personal debt, and restricted access to health services, especially preventive care. This is why other developed countries as different as the United Kingdom, Canada, France, Germany, and Sweden have adopted universal health coverage as the principal component of their welfare states (Street 2008). It is not hard to understand this situation when we keep in mind what was said above concerning the relationship between citizenship, solidarity, and risk pooling, which are typically related to universal health coverage.

The United States spends more on health-care as a percentage of the GDP than any other developed country (see Table 5.1). Because American society is younger on average than most other developed countries, it is impossible to blame population aging for this spending trend. Although the country's higher per capita GDP is a significant piece of the puzzle, other important factors point to the overly complex nature of the public–private American healthcare system. More specifically, in the United States, a "highly complex and fragmented payment system that weakens the demand side of the health sector and entails high administrative

Table 5.1   Health expenditures in selected developed countries (2006)

Country	Total health expenditure as a percentage of GDP	Percentage of public expenditure	Percentage of private expenditure
Australia	8.7	67.7	32.3
Canada	10.0	70.4	29.6
France	11.0	79.7	20.3
Germany	10.6	76.9	23.1
Japan	8.1	81.3	18.7
Sweden	9.2	81.7	18.3
Switzerland	10.8	59.1	40.9
UK	8.2	87.3	12.7
USA	15.3	45.8	54.2

Source: Adapted from World Health Organization, *World Health Statistics 2009*: http://www.who.int/whosis/whostat/2009/en/index.html

costs" (Reinhardt, Hussey, and Anderson 2004: 10) leads to a massive cost-control problem, as sheer institutional complexity and loose government regulations make it much harder than in most other developed nations to control health-care expenditure.

The increase in health-care spending, combined with the lack of universal coverage, is one of the most crucial issues as far as the future of the American welfare state is concerned. In 2009–10, the passionate health-care debate that took place in the United States centered on these two related issues. On one hand, President Obama claimed that it was necessary to finally make health-care coverage accessible to the uninsured while improving the plight of those who already have coverage but fear losing it at any time. For example, the president and other federal officials promised to massively increase coverage and force insurance companies to cover individuals who have a pre-existing medical condition. On the other hand, Obama framed reform efforts as an attempt to control the rapid increase in medical costs, in both the public and the private sectors (Obama 2009). An especially controversial aspect of the president's proposals was the so-called "public option," which would allow the federal government to compete directly against private insurance companies by selling insurance coverage to individuals and families at lower prices. According to the supporters of this approach, the "public option" would increase the level of health insurance coverage while forcing health insurance companies to lower their prices, which would result in large financial savings (Hacker 2008). Opponents of the "public option" saw it as an expensive scheme that would further increase federal deficits while paving the road to a full "government takeover" that, in their opinion, would inevitably reduce the quality of health-care available (Cannon 2009). Actually, in 2009 and early 2010, the health-care debate became overly contentious as conservatives depicted many Democratic proposals as "socialist" and anti-American. This over-the-top rhetoric should not hide the powerful economic issues at stake as well as the related mobilization of health interest groups such as insurance and pharmaceutical companies, which exerted strong pressures on the president and members of Congress, including those who had received large campaign contributions from them in recent years. As in the past (Quadagno 2005), vested interests mobilized to constrain reform efforts, which is consistent with the idea that private benefits and their supporters can strongly impact public policy debates (Hacker 2002).

In late 2009, the idea of a "public option" was not included in the Senate bill adopted just before Christmas, which exacerbated the tension within Democratic ranks. A few weeks later, the unanticipated election in Massachusetts of Republican Scott Brown to the Senate altered the balance of power in the Senate by ending the Democratic "super majority" in place since the 2008 federal election (sixty votes when counting the two independents caucusing with Democrats). Brown took over the seat that Democratic Senator Ted Kennedy, a strong proponent of universal health insurance, had held for more than forty-five years before dying from brain cancer in August 2009. Although he still pushed for health-care reform, in the State of the Union address he gave not long after Brown's surprising victory, President Obama significantly altered his policy agenda in the aftermath of Brown's victory to focus on issues like job creation and fiscal policy (Obama 2010). Yet, after some reluctance to act, the president and his Democratic allies in Congress finally decided to push for legislative action in order for the House to pass the Senate bill as well as "reconciliation" changes aimed at improving it. Although the official death of the "public option" infuriated progressives, most Democrats in the House ended up agreeing that the Senate bill as tweaked by "reconciliation" changes was "better than nothing," especially considering that many of them faced the prospect of a tough re-election battle in the forthcoming (November 2010) mid-term elections. On March 21, the House enacted the Senate bill and a list of changes to it that was later sent to the Senate for approval. President Obama signed the Senate bill into law on March 23, and the "reconciliation" bill featuring the House "fixes" on March 30 (CNN 2010).

Without doubt, the 2010 health reform is the most comprehensive piece of health-care legislation in the United States since the creation of Medicare and Medicaid in 1965. Since the Truman era, the fight for comprehensive health-care reform has mobilized citizens and key interest groups like the American Medical Association (AMA), the pharmaceutical industry, as well as private insurance companies (Klein 2003; Quadagno 2005), and the 2010 reform was no exception. Moreover, Republicans strongly opposed comprehensive reform, and no Republican in Congress ended up voting for the Senate bill or the House "fixes." Within the Democratic House Caucus, deals on issues like abortion were necessary to enact the legislation, and Present Obama even issued an executive order to state that no federal money would be used to fund abortion procedures (except when the life of the mother is at stake, or in case of rape or incest). More generally, the health-care debate was overly passionate, and the 2010 reform is likely to remain controversial for a long time, as both conservatives and progressives dislike major aspects of it. For instance, conservatives typically argue that the legislation is too costly, while progressives lament the absence of a "public option." More generally, like many laws enacted in the United States, the 2010 reform is the product of many legislative compromises, which explains why few experts and policymakers seem entirely satisfied with it.

Considering the complexity of the American health-care system, predicting the long-term impact of the 2010 legislation on issues like health-care costs is hard, as many factors can affect such policy outcomes. However, the broad consequences of this imposing piece of legislation become clear when we start discussing its key provisions, which take place gradually over an eight-year period (2010–18).[3] (The following discussion features only a partial list of these many provisions.) First, in 2010, children are allowed to stay on their parents' health insurance plan until they turn twenty-six. Also, insurance companies can no longer exclude children with a pre-existing health condition. Second, in 2013, new taxes primarily affecting wealthier Americans will kick in to help fund other aspects of the legislation. Third, in 2014, some of the most transformative aspects of the legislation will take effect. For instance, insurance companies will no longer be allowed to deny coverage to adults with pre-existing health conditions like diabetes and high blood pressure. And, starting in 2014, health-care coverage will become mandatory (except for some low-income categories), and people who fail to purchase coverage must pay fines, which will vary according to their income, with wealthier Americans paying higher fines than their poorer counterparts. As for people under age sixty-five with an income up to 33 percent above the poverty line, they will be entitled to Medicaid benefits, a situation that represents a major expansion of this social assistance program. Subsidies will also be created to help low- and middle-income citizens pay for their health coverage. Still in 2014, employers with at least fifty employees who do not provide health insurance coverage to their workers will have to pay a new fine. Finally, the same year, health insurance exchanges will be created to help small businesses and workers who have no employer-granted health coverage to shop for private insurance. Fourth, in 2018, as a cost-control measure, the federal government will also impose a 40 percent tax on so-called "Cadillac plans" that cost far more than the average health-care plan. In addition to the above measures, as a consequence of the 2010 reform, changes to Medicare will be implemented to control costs and improve drug coverage for seniors. Finally, over time, subsidies to small businesses will be implemented to help them provide coverage to their workers.

Overall, this legislation should considerably reduce the number of uninsured, gradually bringing down the proportion of uncovered Americans to about 5 percent of the population. Because the uninsured represented more than 15 percent of the population as of early 2010, this is clearly a major step forward as far as expanding health-care coverage is concerned. However, it is clear that the legislation is unlikely to solve all the major problems facing the American health-care system. For instance, although the reform should improve the long-term fiscal standing of Medicare, another reform is likely to become necessary to truly fix the program's long-term cost-control and financing issues. The same remark applies to private health-care spending, which is hard to control, especially in the absence of a "public option." In general, sooner or later, other important measures should become necessary at the federal and at the state level to further improve the American health-care system. Considering the scope of these issues and the weight of the interest groups that mobilize in the health-care field, in the United States as in other developed countries, the politics of health-care reform should remain contentious for the years and decades to come.

Democracy and Inequality

As stated in Chapter 1, reducing inequality and fostering a more equal citizenry have long been described as defining aspects of modern social policy (Marshall 1964). Today in the United States, this egalitarian undertaking is facing bold challenges. The first challenge involves the persistence of widespread gender, ethnic, and racial inequalities. Although progress has been made since the 1960s, in a report on the relationship between democracy and inequality in the United States, a political science panel formulates a sobering assessment of enduring ethnic and racial income disparities:

> Even as the absolute economic circumstances of minorities have improved, the median white household earned 62 percent more income and possessed twelvefold more wealth than the median black household, with nearly two-thirds of black households (61 percent) and half of Hispanic households lacking any financial assets, as compared with only a quarter of their white counterparts. Even young, married, black couples in which both adults work – the shining beacons of progress toward racial equality – still earn 20 percent less income than their white counterparts and possess a staggering 80 percent less net worth. (American Political Science Association 2004: 2–3)

As for gender inequality, although the wage gap between women and men declined over the last few decades, it remains significant. A recent study on full-time workers judged that the wage gap in 1998 remained as high as 20 percent (Blau and Kahn 2006: 44). Perhaps of more importance, "41 percent of the gender gap cannot be explained even when gender differences in education, experience, industries, occupations, and union status are taken into account. . . . Thus, . . . women earn less than similar men even

138

when all measured characteristics are taken into account" (Blau and Kahn 2006: 44). These remarks suggest that gender discrimination and factors like the unequal division of labor between men and women in terms of housework and child-care explain at least part of the wage gap (Blau and Kahn 2006: 61). Overall, gender inequality, like ethnic and racial inequality, remains a central feature of the American social and economic landscape.

The second challenge concerns social class. Income inequality between the rich and the rest of the American population is on the rise. Related to changing market conditions and, over the last three decades, the ideological prevalence of conservative economic and fiscal ideas, this increase in income inequality is related to the strengthening of business power. Writing about the American situation, Larry Bartels (2008) illustrates that, since the mid-1970s, the rich have truly become richer:

> The share of income going to the rich remained remarkably constant from the mid-1940s through the 1970s and then began to escalate rapidly. For example, the top 5% of taxpayers accounted for 23.0% of total income in 1981 but 37.2% in 2005. The top 1% accounted for 10.0% of total income in 1981 but 21.8% in 2005. After declining gradually over most of the twentieth century, their share of the pie more than doubled in the course of a single generation. (pp. 11–12)

During the same period, low-income families (i.e., the twentieth percentile) faced economic stagnation, as their real income barely increased over the last three decades (Bartels 2008: 9). This situation looks especially dire when American data on income trends are compared with the situation in other developed countries. Consider, for example, this comparison between Britain, France, and the United States:

> The proportion of income accruing to the top one-tenth of one percent of families ran along parallel tracks for much of the 20th century. All three countries reduced inequality from the end of World War I through World War II and until the 1960s. But from the mid-1970s on, the United States rapidly diverged from its two allies and became far more unequal. By 1998, the share of income held by the very rich

was two or three times higher in the United States than in Britain and France. (American Political Science Association 2004: 3)

In other words, compared both to the post-war period and to the current situation in other developed societies, the United States has failed to tackle growing income inequality.

For Bartels (2008), this growing income inequality in the United States is directly related to democratic issues, such as the limited political participation of the poor and the fact that, in a political system where money plays such a key role, elected officials tend to pay much more attention to the grievances of wealthier citizens. The fact that poor citizens are not equally represented in the political arena creates conditions for increasingly regressive fiscal decisions, such as the massive federal tax cuts enacted in 2001 and 2003, which disproportionally favored the wealthy: "These disparities in representation are especially troubling because they suggest the potential for a debilitating feedback cycle linking the economic and political realms: increasing economic inequality may produce increasing inequality in political responsiveness, which in turn produces public policies that are increasingly detrimental to the interests of poor citizens, which in turn produces even greater inequality, and so on" (Bartells 2008: 286). Clearly, income inequality is largely shaped by major political decisions about tax and social policy. And, because the current American political system often favors the wealthy, political reform impacting the "rules of the game" like party financing is one potential aspect of the solution to the country's income inequality problem. Overall, alongside the other challenges discussed above, growing income inequality is a *political* threat to democratic and citizenship inclusion that shall remain central to contemporary debates on the future of social policy. In these debates, it should be recognized that fiscal and tax policy issues are directly related to the welfare state, which is only one possible tool of social redistribution. To reduce inequalities, social programs must work in sync with progressive tax policies. As Barack Obama explained to the individual nicknamed "Joe the Plumber" during the 2008 American presidential campaign, one of the main roles of the state is to "spread the wealth around." Given the Republican attacks launched against the Democratic candidate for simply alluding to a major aspect of modern state action (*Washington Post* 2008), the ideological battle over fiscal redistribution is far from over and is likely to remain on the American agenda for some time to come.

From this discussion, it is clear that the United States is characterized by higher levels of inequality than most other developed countries (American Political Science Association 2004). But, will this always be the case, or is a more egalitarian American economic and social model possible? The best way to answer these questions is to return to our four theories of welfare state development and use examples from the past to speculate on future path-breaking change in the United States. By focusing on the economic and demographic factors central to industrialism, one may argue that a major economic shock similar to the Great Depression could radically increase the political and social pressure on elected officials to tackle inequality and protect workers and citizens against widespread insecurity and massive market failures. In light of what happened during the New Deal era and considering the scope of the 2008 financial crisis, this scenario is not as utopian as some observers may believe. From a historical institutionalist standpoint, it is possible to imagine that, over time, incremental changes such as the expansion of initially small programs like EITC could, as a feedback effect, create stronger political constituencies, which, in turn, could mobilize a more aggressive expansion of the federal welfare state. In terms of the power resource approach, it is possible that the American labor movement may find a way to reorganize that allows it to expand, gather more support in the service sector, and perhaps even regain the strong political voice it has largely lost since the 1970s. General changes in the economic and political landscape could spark the movement's political rejuvenation, and that, in conjunction with other factors, could help trigger a new wave of welfare state expansion in the United States. Finally, from an ideational standpoint, we should reject a static vision of culture and recognize that, over time, well-organized actors can alter the meaning of symbols and values that help justify concrete social policy developments. As mentioned earlier, since the 1970s, conservatives have successfully created influential think thanks and media outlets to help spread their worldview; more recently, a growing number of progressive think tanks and media have emerged to challenge the conservative worldview (Rich 2004).

Only time will tell if one or a combination of factors related to the four theories – or factors not even mentioned here – will produce change that alters the path of contemporary American society, in the sense of a more egalitarian and redistributive welfare state. This welfare state could be more effective at fighting inequality and insecurity while reducing the dependency of workers and citizens on market outcomes and private benefits. Although incremental change is a likely scenario, the possibility of sudden, radical change should never be discounted by students of social policy – the history of the New Deal is there to remind us of this possibility. But to take this possibility seriously, we must discard the myth that globalization has reduced the power of the national state to the point it is now impossible to enact meaningful and consequential policies dictated by citizens and collective national actors, rather than by transnational corporations. Even when recognizing that national states remain largely autonomous in terms of welfare state development, to really think about the long-term future of social policy, we can turn to the contemporary debate on globalization for insight into the transnational context and its potential impact on national welfare states. Here we must take a truly global perspective and, at first, focus less on the United States than in some of the previous sections.

Globalization and Social Policy

Defining Globalization

Since the 1990s, many students of social policy have debated the impact of globalization on national welfare states (e.g., Deacon 2007; Huber and Stephens 2001; Iversen 2005; Mishra 1999; Swank 2002; Yeates 2001; for an overview of the debate see

Genschel 2004).[4] Globalization is a broad sociological concept that refers not only to global trade and finance, but also to issues ranging from immigration to the development of the Internet and other communication technologies. Globalization is not a new phenomenon, but it has accelerated in recent decades (Giddens 1990). According to Mauro Guillén (2001), globalization is "a process fueled by, and resulting in, increasing cross-border flows of goods, services, money, people, information, and culture," flows that favor a "shrinking of the world" (p. 236). Although it is clear that globalization is an influential process, "global relations have spread unevenly across regions and social sectors" and "globalization is a thoroughly political question, significantly overpowering some and disempowering others" (Scholte 2002: 4). For example, in the field of social policy, it is possible to argue that economic globalization has increased business power, partly because the threat of relocation and/or financial withdrawal can impact the decisions of national social policy actors (Huber and Stephens 2001). Despite this, it is clear that, in developed societies at least, the national state remains the most crucial source of social protection (Béland 2007). Around the world, national actors remain central to welfare state politics (Orenstein 2008). This remark particularly applies to the United States, the most powerful country on earth, where domestic actors and forces like federalism, electoral politics, and interest group mobilization remain more central to the politics of the welfare state than global economic and fiscal pressures.

Overall, the impact of particular aspects of globalization on the welfare state varies a lot from one country to another. For instance, compared to the United States, some countries, especially poor ones, are far more subject to financial pressures from international organizations. But where developed countries are concerned, there is no evidence that globalization, in itself, has strongly weakened national welfare states (Castles 2004; Huber and Stephens 2001; Swank 2002). In the United States and in other developed countries, domestic actors and institutions typically remain the most central forces behind policy development, which does not, however, mean that transnational actors and processes do not matter in any significant way (Campbell 2004; Orenstein 2008). In fact, as suggested below, although globalization does not favor welfare state decline in developed societies, several of the key social policy challenges they face today stem largely from concrete transnational processes related to globalization.

Global Challenges

The first global challenge we will discuss is the enduring nature of the inequalities between developed and developing countries. Scholars are divided over the nature of recent changes in global economic disparities. For example, according to expert David Dollar (2007), "growth rates of developing economies have accelerated and are higher than those of industrialized countries; the number of extremely poor people (those living with less than $1 a day) has declined for the first time in history . . . ; measures of global inequality . . . have declined modestly, reversing a long historical trend towards greater inequality" (p. 80). But other scholars argue that, in the 1980s and 1990s, instead of declining, global inequality increased significantly (Milanovic 2005). Beyond this major debate on the direction of change, the scope of global income inequality remains massive by any standard: "The top 5 per cent of individuals in the world receive about 1/3 of total world (PPP-valued) income, and the top 10 per cent get one-half. If we take the bottom 5 and 10 per cent, they receive 0.2 and 0.7 per cent of total world income respectively" (Milanovic 2006: 9). In addition to the global income inequalities between individuals, there are enormous economic and social disparities between countries. From GDP per capita to infant mortality and rates of alphabetization (i.e., one's capacity to read and write), global inequalities between nations and regions of the world are hard to overstate (e.g., Cohen and Kennedy 2000). As for the debate on the causes of such inequalities, this is typically between those who stress cultural and social factors specific to each country (Rostow 1990) and those who focus mainly on structural forces (i.e., the unequal exchange at the center of global capitalism) that prevent many poorer countries from moving up the global economic ladder (Wallerstein 1974).

For our purposes, the goal is not to explain global inequalities but to understand their consequences for the welfare state in developed countries such as the United States. One consequence is that debates on global trade, especially trade between developed and developing countries, increasingly involve labor and social policy issues. For example, a significant aspect of recent trade negotiations was the enforcement of labor standards and social rights. Labor unions and left-leaning politicians have long protested the exclusion of labor standards from major international trade agreements. This was the case in the early 1990s during the negotiations leading to the enactment of the North American Free Trade Agreement (NAFTA) between the United States, Canada, and Mexico: "Prominent among the objections to the NAFTA were concerns that labor standards are not enforced at a sufficiently high level in Mexico, and therefore that the competition that will ensue from the NAFTA will place US domestic industries at a disadvantage vis-à-vis their Mexican competitors" (Brown, Deardorff, and Stern 1996: 227). The policy debate over NAFTA is far from over – during the 2008 Democratic primaries, both Barack Obama and Hillary Clinton raised the issue of labor standards and even the possibility of negotiating with Canada and Mexico to improve NAFTA (Malkin 2008).

Beyond NAFTA, the status of labor standards and social rights within trade agreements is likely to remain on the agenda of ongoing trade negotiations between developed nations such as the United States and developing countries such as China and India. It is likely because many labor advocates living in developed countries fear that the lack of comprehensive labor and social standards in trade agreements is pushing major firms to relocate to developing countries, where much lower standards could increase their profit margins. From a political standpoint, what is certain is that financial and trade globalization has empowered many businesses, using the threat of relocation, to increase pressure on governments to accommodate their demands for lower taxes and even reduced social protection for workers (Huber and Stephens 2001: 224).

A second consequence of global inequalities is that, just like wars and human rights violations, global economic disparities are a key

145

force behind migrations of people from the "Global South" who are attempting to find a better life for themselves and their children in wealthier, developed countries such as the United States.[5] Immigration has a very long history, but, with the rapid increase in the world's population (from 2.5 billion inhabitants in 1950 to more than 6.7 billion in 2009) and the enduring nature of global inequalities, demographic pressures tied to global migration flows are likely to increase. Because of the lower fertility rates and the accelerated demographic aging that characterize many developed societies, increasing immigration quotas could help these societies tackle their demographic challenge. Even in Japan, a wealthy country with unusually restrictive immigration and naturalization policies, the idea of welcoming and retaining a greater number of immigrants to offset the negative economic and fiscal impact of population decline is gaining ground (Harden 2009).

In other countries, however, it is illegal immigration that has become a major issue. This is the case in the United States, which shares a 2,000-mile land border with Mexico, a much poorer country that has had massive population growth in recent decades. In comparison, Canada is relatively unaffected by this issue, since it only shares a (long) land border with the United States, an unlikely source of massive illegal immigration (Kymlicka 2005). In the United States, the ideologically charged debate on illegal immigration is directly related to social policy issues. For instance, some nativist politicians depict illegal immigrants as a drain on the country's welfare programs. However, according to Shikha Dalmia (2006), this claim is false because "the 1996 welfare reform bill disqualified illegal immigrants from nearly all means-tested government programs including food stamps, housing assistance, Medicaid and Medicare-funded hospitalization. The only services that illegals can still get are emergency medical care and K-12 education." This limited social coverage contributes to the fact that illegal immigrants suffer from greater economic insecurity than the rest of the American population. Moreover, as opposed to what most people believe, "two-thirds of illegal immigrants pay Medicare, Social Security and personal income taxes" (Dalmia 2006). Overall, illegal immigration remains a central policy issue that requires attention. Allowing illegal immigrants who have lived in the United States for years to remain in the country is an idea that has been widely discussed by advocates and politicians, but, as revealed by the debate on immigration policy during President George W. Bush's second term (2005–9), there is significant opposition to this solution.

Beyond the issue of illegal immigrants, social policy and immigration are connected in part because the state must determine who is eligible to receive welfare and other types of benefits, a question that relates to citizenship and national identity (Banting and Kymlicka 2007). Considering the enduring scope of global inequalities, it is unlikely that transnational migratory pressures will sharply decline anytime soon. Thus, future social policy debates may feature immigration issues prominently, as citizens and politicians argue over both immigration quotas and social benefits for newcomers. As demonstrated by the 1996 welfare reform, which stripped most future immigrants (i.e., non-citizens) of their access to Medicaid and social assistance, even social benefits for *legal* immigrants are vulnerable to cutbacks (Benson Gold 2003). Yet, interestingly, a public backlash forced federal policymakers to withdraw provisions that would have penalized immigrants who had settled in the United States prior to Congress passing the 1996 reform (Schuck 2001: 117–18). In the end, because social programs can reduce inequalities and reinforce social solidarity, the anti-immigrant bias in social policy could have dire long-term consequences for immigrant integration and the promotion of cultural diversity. Given that about 11 percent of Americans were born abroad (Benson Gold 2003), the fate of immigrants within the welfare state is likely to remain on the social policy agenda for years and decades to come.

A third consequence of global inequalities concerns foreign aid that wealthier countries provide to developing nations, partly for diplomatic reasons that influence their own policies and partly to help these nations modernize their economies, address large humanitarian crises, and improve the well-being of their population (Lancaster 2006).[6] To a certain extent, foreign aid is the international extension of the welfare state, as it highlights the commitment of developed countries to support poorer countries. In that regard, the correlation between levels of foreign aid and domestic social spending is particularly intriguing. For example, social-democratic countries with comprehensive and universalistic social programs, such as Norway and Sweden, tend to spend a greater proportion of their GDP on foreign aid than countries belonging to the conservative and liberal welfare regimes. From this perspective, there is a relationship between national solidarity expressed through universal social programs and commitment to foreign aid and international solidarity (Noël and Thérien 1995). It is not surprising, then, to learn that, compared to other developed countries, the United States does poorly when national levels of foreign aid are assessed. In fact, "out of the United States' GDP, just 0.16 percent is allocated to foreign aid, among the lowest percentage of G-8 members" (Beehner 2005). Because social-democratic countries are likely to keep their foreign aid spending at higher levels than their American counterpart, for advocates of global social justice, the implicit message is that national struggles for more comprehensive social programs in developed countries may be directly related to the quest for greater international solidarity. To a certain extent, standards of solidarity and social justice that are dominant at home typically extend to foreign aid, thus building more extensive and redistributive social programs for your citizens does not necessarily contradict the quest for international solidarity.

Finally, with the help of academics, think tanks, and international organizations such as the European Union and the World Bank, policy ideas can rapidly spread from one country to another (Béland 2010; Deacon 2007; Orenstein 2008). However, even though many policy ideas spread beyond borders, when country-level policies is concerned, national boundaries and political institutions remain at the center of the policymaking process (Campbell 2004). Moreover, despite the advent of large transnational policy networks (Stone 2008), in each country, national institutions continue to structure the production of policy expertise (Campbell and Pedersen 2010). Finally, even in developing countries, under most circumstances, international organizations collaborate with national bureaucrats and politicians to secure the adoption – and the successful implementation – of the policy ideas they promote (Orenstein 2008).

As well as international organizations, in the United States, think tanks can contribute to the global diffusion of policy ideas through their promotion of specific "foreign models" aimed at influencing the course of national policy debates. For example, since the 1980s, supporters of Social Security privatization have discussed the apparent virtues of the "Chilean model" of pension reform, which was implemented during the Pinochet dictatorship on the advice of conservative economists interested in propagating their market ideas around the world (Béland and Waddan 2000). Also, during the 2009–10 American health-care debate, much was said about the perceived flaws and virtues of foreign health-care systems, notably the British and the Canadian ones (e.g., Clark 2009).

Policy diffusion is a two-way street and policy ideas travel in and out of particular countries with the help of actors who must translate these ideas into their own national – cultural and political – language (Campbell 2004). With the development of modern communication technologies like the Internet, the transnational diffusion of policy ideas is much easier to achieve today than in the past. Yet, in general, national cultures and institutions tend to mediate the implementation of these ideas by forcing national actors to adapt them (Campbell 2004). Thus, although the role of transnational factors is impossible to deny, the welfare state remains a territorial construction tied to national actors, borders, cultures, and institutions.

Conclusion

Because it is difficult for social scientists to forecast the future, this chapter has simply attempted to map some of the key challenges that could significantly impact social policy in the years ahead. In the United States as in other developed countries, these challenges include changing labor markets, demographic aging, growing health-care costs as well as rising insecurity and inequality. Additionally, global forces create challenges of their own; but, although these forces can impact them in significant ways, in developed countries, national welfare states have thus far proved surprisingly resilient (Castles 2004). Overall, the welfare state faces serious challenges, but there is no evidence that it is a doomed institution facing an irremediable decline.

We can only speculate about what *could* happen in the future. From unforeseen and dramatic economic fluctuations to surprising political twists and turns, few of us could accurately predict such things even a few months in advance. Yet, what we know for sure is that, as evidenced throughout this chapter, many of the processes likely to shape social policy in contemporary societies are inherently *political* in nature. Keeping this reality in mind is essential to understanding the contemporary debates about the future of the welfare state.

Conclusion

Social policy is a complex and multifaceted topic, but I hope that this short book has helped you gain a comparative, historical, and political perspective on it. As made clear in previous chapters, social programs directly affect us in one way or another, and we are likely to rely on the welfare state during key moments of our life: when we feel the least secure, when social and economic problems hit us in the face, often unexpectedly. Keeping this in mind, it is now time to draw a few more general lessons from the book's five chapters before we discuss the implications of social policy research for the future of the welfare state and what is known as "public sociology."

What Have We Learned?

Many lessons may be drawn from the material in this book. Because most of them are discussed in detail in the chapters, only those that concern what social policy is and how we should study it are emphasized here.

First, the concept of social policy refers to a number of distinct program types and policy areas that perform several interrelated tasks, ranging from poverty alleviation and risk pooling to de-commodification and citizenship inclusion. The institutional boundaries of social policy and, more generally, state intervention are disputed, and it is problematic to adopt a narrow vision of the welfare state, as it deals with major economic, social, and political issues such as citizenship, economic development, and democratic participation. Instead of focusing exclusively on narrow issues and policy details that, although important, are merely branches on the social policy tree, we must keep the "big picture" in mind.

Second, any analysis of the American welfare state must consider two major forms of policy fragmentation: (1) the development of private social benefits and (2) the territorial logic of federalism. On one hand, private benefits pose unique challenges in terms of social inequality and political regulation, as the state plays a lower-profile yet essential role in both promoting and regulating numerous private schemes. On the other hand, federalism empowers regional actors while creating major governance challenges that directly impact the politics of the welfare state. More generally, beyond the issue of federalism, social programs have a territorial dimension, hence questions like centralization and decentralization feature in many social policy debates.

Third, to understand social policy, we need to gain a historical, comparative, and political perspective on welfare state development and restructuring. The welfare state is a social and political construction, the empirical content of which varies from one country to another and from one historical moment to another. More important, the way in which political decisions about social programs unfold over time can help explain differences between countries and between policy areas within the same country. In the case of the United States, the emphasis on comparative research is especially important because looking at it is necessary to understand both what is common and what is specific about American social programs. Although exceptional in many respects, the American case is easier to understand in the broader context of the liberal welfare regime and, more generally, in light of the comparative literature on welfare state development and restructuring. Because the national state remains the focal point of modern social policy, it is absolutely legitimate for scholars, students, and citizens to focus on their own country. Yet, we can learn a great deal from other countries, and when we do so, we are likely to learn about ourselves, too. This is as true in the United States as anywhere else in the world.

Fourth, in developed countries, recent changes in social policy follow several major patterns, such as "activation" and the push for fiscal control that is present across the developed world. But, this general observation does not mean that a systematic and enduring form of international convergence is taking place or that key differences between countries are disappearing altogether. Time-frame is a crucial aspect of social policy analysis and of social science analysis in general. As noted in Chapter 4, although it is probably too soon to draw definite conclusions about the "convergence debate," undertaking new research on the topic remains crucial, and time-frame considerations should be central to studies on convergence and policy change.

Fifth, although it is clear that the trends discussed in Chapter 5 are important, we should remain open-minded about what the future may look like, because studies on the history of social policy suggest that change is largely the product of the contingent inter-action between the causal factors identified by the four theories of welfare state development discussed in Chapter 3. In other words, although we can easily map potential causal factors and looming policy issues, it is much more difficult to imagine how they will interact in the future, for the simple reason that twists and turns abound in social policy as in any other aspect of human history. In the mid-1920s, for example, few Americans – including the best economists of the time – predicted that an unprecedented economic catastrophe such as the Great Depression would occur a few years later. Political dramas and surprise electoral results can also reconfigure the interaction between well-known forces, which in turn may produce path-departing change over time. Furthermore, cultural values and social institutions like the family are not purely static. They can evolve without creating much fuss, until people begin to notice what has changed – years and even decades after key changes have begun to unfold. Being aware of the broad empirical trends and theories discussed in this book should not prevent us from recognizing potentially surprising events that could reshape the meaning of those trends and theories. At the same time, although having the "big picture" in mind is crucial for understanding social policy and explaining welfare state politics, the "big picture" is a changing reality and we should regularly revisit our core assumptions about how the world works, because this is how we will notice unexpected trends when they occur.

Finally, one lesson conveyed throughout this book is that the welfare state is a political reality that can both reflect and challenge existing forms of inequality. In the early post-World War II era, most social scientists interested in the welfare state were white males who focused mainly on class politics and on people who looked like them. Although class politics remains relevant, today's social policy scholars form a more diverse crowd and, in recent decades, have paid increasing attention to other forms of inequality. Prominent among these traditionally neglected forms of social inequality are gender, race, and ethnicity. As with class, these categories are social constructions related to concrete power relations that affect political debates on social programs. Sometimes, gendered and racial categories are explicitly put forward in such debates but, in other cases, they are located in the unspoken background of prejudice. This is especially true when race is involved, since most people are afraid to express openly racist views in public, which was not necessarily the case fifty or sixty years ago. As a result, instead of disappearing altogether, racial prejudice has moved to the background of many public debates (Trepagnier 2006). In addition to gender, race, and ethnicity, sexual orientation has recently become a prominent social policy issue: for example, in the field of health-care services (Wilton 2000). Only time will tell how prominent a role issues related to sexual orientation – such as access to spousal benefits for same-sex couples – will have in future policy debates. What is certain at this point is that, in our world, social policy debates are related to identity issues and the politics of inequality surrounding them. In turn, these identity issues are related to a broader struggle against discrimination, which can range from unequal laws to subtle forms of harassment and biases present at the bureaucratic, service-delivery level.

Overall, although social programs and policy decisions about them may reflect existing patterns of social inequality, they can also challenge them by reducing key forms of inequality and by increasing the level of de-commodification, social solidarity, and citizenship inclusion. However, for the welfare state to reduce inequalities, rather than simply reflecting or even increasing them, major political battles must take place. The goal of this book's discussions on how social programs and the politics of the welfare state work was to increase your awareness of the political nature of the welfare state and the forms of inequality and insecurity it can fight. Although the disadvantaged are more in need of state support than other citizens, social policy is not just about the poor – social insecurity and market failures can affect most of us, and because we pay for social programs in one way or another, we are involved in their development.

Among other things, the welfare state is about redistribution, and it features large fiscal transfers. Paying taxes is a duty of citizenship and, as Justice Oliver Wendell Holmes famously claimed, taxes are "what we pay for a civilized society." Indeed, this is precisely why citizens typically want to ensure that tax money is used effectively and in accordance with their values. Defining the meaning and consequences of these shared values is a significant aspect of the politics of social policy and partly why this book emphasizes the role of ideas and culture in policy change. In general, welfare state politics is centered on trade-offs between debated policy options and the resources available to finance them. Accounting for fiscal trade-offs and exploring the ideas that give meaning to them are essential to the advent of more enlightened public debates on social policy reform and its impact on citizenship, economic insecurity, and social inequality.

Why Should We Care?

Why should social scientists care about the welfare state, exactly? Too often, social policy is perceived as an overly technical field of study that is distinct from and less valuable than other types of social science research.[1] This book suggests that interesting social science analysis and welfare state research are not only compatible but they can even feed one another. This suggestion is especially important in an era of growing economic insecurity and social inequality. In this context, social scientists interested in the welfare state are in a good position to inform the political debates of our time.

At a more general level, there are two main reasons why social scientists should take the welfare state seriously. First, the creation and expansion of the welfare state during the twentieth century has meant that, today, social policy is a major aspect of our lives. Indeed, in our society, it is impossible to study many social and political processes without explicitly taking into account social programs and the reconfigurations of the relationship between the state and other social institutions such as the family and the economic system. Second, with the growing interest in "public sociology," which stresses the active role social scientists can take in public debates (Blau and Iyall Smith 2006; Burawoy 2005; Clawson et al. 2007; Nichols 2007), it is easier for us to move the relationship between social science analysis and social policy beyond a technocratic model centered exclusively on technical problem solving. Here, we must fully acknowledge the political nature of the policy debates in which we can participate. This applies to professors and other professional researchers, as well as to university students and ordinary citizens who want to make a difference. Having more knowledge about our world does not mean one can change it overnight, but it is a precondition for effective political action and sound policy debates. Although we must always remain conscious of the limits of our knowledge, studying social programs from a comparative, historical, and political perspective is a useful and legitimate way to contribute to debates on the future of the welfare state in these times of economic and social uncertainty. And, because new ideas are more likely to become influential in times of economic and political uncertainty (Blyth 2002), current social policy debates may prove extremely influential. In light of this, the question is: will we seize this opportunity to have our voices heard and help reshape the welfare state according to our hopes and values?

Notes

Introduction

1 Throughout this book, the word "state" is used in the European sense, which is dominant in comparative and international social policy research. This concept refers to a set of territorially bounded institutions that makes and enforces the rules governing society (Hall and Ikenberry 1989: 1–2). In the United States, this set of institutions is typically known as "government."

2 For introductions to social policy not centered on the United States, see Blackmore 1998; Dean 2007; Hill 2003. Most introductions to American social policy are written from a social work perspective: e.g., Jansson 2009; Popple and Neighninger 2003; van Wormer 2006. For a European reader devoted to social policy research, see Pierson and Castles 2006.

Chapter 1 Social Policy and the Welfare State

1 The British Social Policy Association (SPA) is a professional organization that publishes several major journals, including the *Journal of Social Policy* (http://www.social-policy.com/).

2 On the work of T. H. Marshall, see Kymlicka and Norman 1995; Turner 1993.

3 In France and other European countries such as Belgium and Germany, social insurance systems are fragmented among occupational groups, which is not the case in American social insurance programs such as Social Security (Baldwin 1990).

4 Throughout this book, the post-war era refers to the period of economic expansion that ran from 1945 to the mid-1970s.

5 For a systematic discussion of this issue, see Béland 2007. For a different (and French) take on state protection, see Rosanvallon 1990.

6 Some Canadian provinces still collect formal health contributions, but people who do not or cannot pay them remain entitled to health-care services, which

are accessible to all citizens and permanent residents. For example, under the Canada Health Act (1984), people moving from one province to another are immediately entitled to health benefits in the new province, regardless of their contribution record (in the case of the few provinces that still have contributions).
7 On the history of the term "welfare" in the United States see, Katz 2008.
8 This paragraph draws extensively on Howard 1997.

Chapter 2 The United States in International Context

1 As Daniel Wincott (2001) convincingly argues, Esping-Andersen's 1990 book, *The Three Worlds of Welfare Capitalism*, is rather vague from a conceptual standpoint, and it refers to the potentially confusing term "welfare state regimes." In his 1999 book, *Social Foundations of Postindustrial Economies*, Esping-Andersen clarified the meaning of his typology of welfare regimes. The following discussion of his work takes this into account instead of stressing the conceptual vagueness present in *The Three Worlds of Welfare Capitalism*.
2 In fact, Esping-Andersen's welfare regime framework has been criticized for not accurately portraying key differences between health-care systems. On this issue, see Padamsee 2007.
3 Although developing countries have been generally ignored in Esping-Andersen's work, scholars have attempted to classify them using new social policy typologies. For example, Michael Kpessa (2009) explores the interface between the state, the market, and the family to map differences in social policy provisions in Sub-Saharan Africa, where social programs are generally limited in scope.
4 Like gender, race and ethnicity are social and historical constructions, not purely biological realities. An important issue is how people perceive racial and ethnic categories and how institutions can reflect the implicit hierarchies they typically feature.
5 For a systematic discussion about these countries, see the various chapters in Béland and Gran 2008.
6 It is worth noting that, under SSI, the states are permitted to supplement federal payments with additional benefits while setting their own policies regarding such benefits.
7 For a broad discussion see Béland and Lecours 2008.
8 For more information on state health-care coverage, see http://www.state coverage.org/

Chapter 3 Welfare State Reform

1 On the history and diffusion of the term "welfare state," see Alber 1988; Flora and Heidenheimer 1981; Petersen and Petersen 2009.

2 For a comprehensive historical overview of American welfare state development, see Berkowitz 1991 and Trattner 1998. A detailed chronology is available at http://www.ssa.gov/history/chrono.html

3 The following paragraphs partly draw on Béland 2005.

4 This led Ira Katznelson (2005) to refer to some of the programs enacted during the 1930s and 1940s as "affirmative action for whites," which is a provocative yet potentially misleading parallel, since the guiding principles of these programs had little to do with what is known today as "affirmative action."

5 Recognizing that the exclusion of agricultural and domestic workers disproportionately affected African Americans and other minorities does not, however, mean that racial prejudice necessarily explains the exclusion of these occupational categories (Davies and Derthick 1997).

6 In the United States, as the recent debate about the creation of a "public option" suggests, the idea of a competition between public and private health insurance has taken a new political meaning (see Chapter 5).

7 The following theoretical overview extensively builds on Béland 2005.

8 In the United States, this approach is related to American Political Development (APD), a recent scholarly tradition that emphasizes the role of historical processes in politics and policy. APD is grounded in the theoretical precept that "because a polity in all its different parts is constructed historically, over time, the nature and prospects of any single part will be best understood within the long course of political formation." (Orren and Skowronek 2004: 1). Owing to its explicit American focus, however, this approach is not central to international debates about comparative welfare state development, which is why it is not surveyed here.

9 Beginning in the 1970s, a growing number of public intellectuals began criticizing what they saw as the excessively bureaucratic nature of the modern welfare state, which they depicted as a major source of social control and dehumanization (Alber 1988: 459).

Chapter 4 Retrenchment and Restructuring

1 It is important to note that, in the United States, the Keynesian model implemented during the post-war years only partially corresponded to the ideas of British economist John Maynard Keynes (Turgeon 1996).

2 Simultaneously, on the left, Marxist authors such as James O'Connor (1973) helped delegitimize the welfare state through their writings on the "fiscal crisis of the state" and their depiction of social programs as tools of capitalist exploitation and reproduction. Despite the genuine differences between them, the conservative and the Marxist critiques of the welfare state have much in common as they both depict it as being inefficient and repressive (Offe 1982, 1984).

3 This paragraph draws extensively on Martin 2008.

4 For more on the difference between blame avoidance and credit claiming, see Weaver 1986; for more on the idea of credit claiming, see Mayhew 1974.

5 For a critical perspective, see Béland 2001.

6 On layering, see also Schickler 2001.

7 The idea of "third way" became influential in the 1990s as a centrist vision aimed at moving beyond the traditional right–left dichotomy. It was especially prominent in the United Kingdom when it was adopted as the slogan of Tony Blair's New Labour. The term is closely associated with the work of British social theorist Anthony Giddens (1994, 1998).

8 The following discussion is based on Béland 2001.

Chapter 5 Looming Challenges

1 For a similar discussion, see Garner 2000: 392.

2 In 2000, based on a different definition of poverty (i.e., living with less than 50 percent of median national income) than the one used by the federal government, nearly 25 percent of Americans aged 65 or older lived in poverty, compared to only 10.1 percent in Germany and 7.7 percent in Sweden. Two years earlier, in Canada, only 7.8 percent of the elderly lived in poverty (Wiseman and Yčas 2008: 54).

3 This paragraph draws extensively on *Wall Street Journal* 2010; see also Kaiser Foundation 2010.

4 For a more systematic discussion of the idea of globalization on which this paragraph draws, see Béland 2007.

5 Additionally, forced migration in the context of human-trafficking networks is a widespread global problem that has clear social policy implications (Zhang 2007).

6 For a critical perspective on American foreign aid that stresses its dark diplomatic side, see Bealinger 2006.

Conclusion

1 The following section partially draws on Béland 2009.

References

Aaron, Henry J., and Robert D. Reischauer. 2001. *Countdown to reform: The great Social Security debate* (Updated Edition). New York: Century Foundation Press.

Abelson, Reed. 2008. "Uninsured put a strain on hospitals." *New York Times*, December 8.

Abrams, Lynn. 2006. *Bismarck and German empire: 1871–1918* (Second Edition). London: Routledge.

Achenbaum, W. Andrew. 1986. *Social security: Visions and revisions*. Cambridge: Cambridge University Press.

Adema, Willem, and Maxime Ladaique. 2005. *Net social expenditure, 2005 edition: More comprehensive measures of social support*. Paris: Organization for Economic Co-operation and Development (OECD).

Albanese, Patrizia. 2006. "Small town, big benefits: The ripple effect of 7/day child care." *Canadian Review of Sociology and Anthropology* 43(2): 125–40.

Alber, Jens. 1988. "Continuities and changes in the idea of the welfare state." *Politics & Society*, 16(4): 451–68.

Altman, Nancy. 2005. *The battle for social security: From FDR's vision to Bush's gamble*. Hoboken, NJ: Wiley.

Altmeyer, Arthur J. 1965. *The formative years of social security*. Madison: University of Wisconsin Press.

Amenta, Edwin. 1998. *Bold relief: Institutional politics and the origins of modern social policy*. Princeton: Princeton University Press.

Amenta, Edwin. 2006. *When movements matter: The Townsend Plan and the rise of social security*. Princeton: Princeton University Press.

Amenta, Edwin, Chris Bonastia, and Neal Caren. 2001. "US social policy in comparative and historical perspective: Concepts, images, arguments, and research strategies." *Annual Review of Sociology* 27: 213–34.

American Political Science Association (Task Force on Inequality and American Democracy). 2004. *American democracy in an age of rising inequality*. Washington, DC: American Political Science Association.

References

Anderson, Karen M. 2005. "Sweden: Radical reform in a mature pension system." In Giuliano Bonoli and Toshimitsu Shinkawa, eds, *Ageing and pension reform around the world*, 94–115. Cheltenham: Edward Elgar.

apRoberts, Lucy. 2000. *Les retraites aux États-Unis: Sécurité sociale et fonds de pension*. Paris: La Dispute.

Armingeon, Klaus, and Giuliano Bonoli, eds. 2006. *The politics of post-industrial welfare states: Adapting post-war social policies to new social risks*. London: Routledge.

Arts, Wil, and John Gelissen. 2006. "Three worlds of welfare capitalism or more? A state-of-the-art report." In Christopher Pierson and Francis G. Castles, eds, *The welfare state reader* (Second Edition), 175–97. Cambridge: Polity.

Ashton, Toni, and Susan St John. 2008. "New Zealand: The expansion of the state in a liberal welfare regime." In Daniel Béland and Brian Gran, eds, *Public and private social policy: Health and pension policies in a new era*, 123–46. Basingstoke: Palgrave Macmillan.

Baker, Dean, and Mark Weisbrot. 1999. *Social Security: The phony crisis*. Chicago: University of Chicago Press.

Baker, Maureen. 2006. *Restructuring family policies: Convergences and divergences*. Toronto: University of Toronto Press.

Baldwin, Peter. 1990. *The politics of social solidarity: Class bases of the European welfare state, 1875–1975*. New York: Cambridge University Press.

Banting, Keith. 1987. *The welfare state and Canadian federalism* (Second Edition). Montreal/Kingston: McGill-Queen's University Press.

Banting, Keith. 2005. "Canada: nation-building in a federal welfare state" in Herbert Obinger, Stephan Leibfried and Frank G. Castles (eds.), *Federalism and the welfare State: new world and European experiences*. Cambridge: Cambridge University Press, pp. 89–137.

Banting, Keith, George Hoberg, and Richard Simeon, eds. 1997. *Degrees of freedom: Canada and the United States in a changing world*. Montreal: McGill-Queen's University Press.

Banting, Keith, and Will Kymlicka. 2007. "Introduction: Multiculturalism and the welfare state: Setting the context." In Keith Banting and Will Kymlicka, eds, *Multiculturalism and the welfare state: Recognition and redistribution in contemporary democracies*, 1–45. Oxford: Oxford University Press.

Barreto, Amilcar Antonio. 2007. "Nationalism at play: Vacillating education and language policies in Puerto Rico." In Katherine Schuster and David Witkosky, eds, *Language of the land: Policy, politics, identity*, 3–24. Charlotte, NC: Information Age Publishing.

Barr, Nicholas. 1993. *The economics of the welfare state* (Second Edition). Stanford: Stanford University Press.

Bartels, Larry. 2008. *Unequal democracy: The political economy of the New Gilded Age*. New York: Russell Sage Foundation; Princeton: Princeton University Press.

162

Bashevkin, Sylvia. 2000. "Rethinking retrenchment: North American social policy during the early Clinton and Chrétien years." *Canadian Journal of Political Science* 33(1): 7–36.

Bealinger, Andrew A., ed. 2006. *Foreign aid: Control, corrupt, contain?* Hauppauge, NY: Nova Publishers.

Beehner, Lionel. 2005. "Africa: Debt-relief proposals." Washington, DC: Council on Foreign Relations. http://www.cfr.org/publication/8167/africa.html (accessed March 18, 2010).

Béland, Daniel. 2001. "Does labor matter? Institutions, labor unions and pension reform in France and the United States." *Journal of Public Policy* 21(2): 153–72.

Béland, Daniel. 2005. *Social security: History and politics from the New Deal to the privatization debate.* Lawrence: University Press of Kansas.

Béland, Daniel. 2007. *States of global insecurity: Policy, politics, and society.* New York: Worth Publishers.

Béland, Daniel. 2009. "Sociology and public policy." *Footnotes* 37(4): 7.

Béland, Daniel. 2010. "Policy change and health care research." *Journal of Health Politics, Policy and Law* 35(3).

Béland, Daniel, and Robert H. Cox, eds. 2010. *Ideas and politics in social science research.* New York: Oxford University Press.

Béland, Daniel, and Brian Gran, eds. 2008. *Public and private social policy: Health and pension policies in a new era.* Basingstoke: Palgrave Macmillan.

Béland, Daniel, and Jacob S. Hacker. 2004. "Ideas, private institutions, and American welfare state 'exceptionalism': The case of health and old-age insurance, 1915–1965." *International Journal of Social Welfare* 13(1): 42–54.

Béland, Daniel, and Randall Hansen. 2000. "Reforming the French welfare state: Solidarity, social exclusion and the three crises of citizenship." *West European Politics* 23(1): 47–64.

Béland, Daniel, and André Lecours. 2008. *Nationalism and social policy: The politics of territorial solidarity.* Oxford: Oxford University Press.

Béland, Daniel, and Patrik Marier. 2006. "The politics of protest avoidance: Labor mobilization and social policy reform in France." *Mobilization: An International Journal* 11(3): 297–311.

Béland, Daniel, and John Myles. 2005. "Stasis amidst change: Canadian pension reform in an age of retrenchment." In Giuliano Bonoli and Toshimitsu Shinkawa, eds, *Ageing and pension reform around the World*, 252–72. Cheltenham: Edward Elgar.

Béland, Daniel, and Toshimitsu Shinkawa. 2007. "Public and private policy change: Pension reform in four countries." *Policy Studies Journal* 35(3): 349–71.

Béland, Daniel, and François Vergniolle de Chantal. 2004. "Fighting 'Big Government': Frames, federalism, and social policy reform in the United States." *Canadian Journal of Sociology* 29(2): 241–64.

References

Béland, Daniel, François Vergniolle de Chantal, and Alex Waddan. 2002. "Third way social policy: Clinton's legacy?" *Policy & Politics* 30(1): 19–30.

Béland, Daniel, and Alex Waddan. 2000. "From Thatcher (and Pinochet) to Clinton? Conservative think tanks, foreign models and US pensions reform." *Political Quarterly* 71(2): 202–10.

Béland, Daniel, and Alex Waddan. 2010a. "The politics of policy change: Welfare, Medicare and Social Security. Unpublished manuscript.

Béland, Daniel, and Alex Waddon. 2010b. "The politics of social policy change: Lessons of the Clinton and Bush presidencies." *Policy & Politics* 38(2): 217–33.

Bell, Daniel. 1973. *The coming of the post-industrial society: A venture in social forecasting.* New York: Basic Books.

Benson Gold, Rachel. 2003. "Immigrants and Medicaid after welfare reform." *The Guttmacher Report on Public Policy* 6(2). http://www.guttmacher.org/pubs/tgr/06/2/gr060206.html (accessed March 18, 2010).

Berkowitz, Edward D. 1983. "The first social security crisis." *Prologue* 15(3): 133–49.

Berkowitz, Edward D. 1987. *Disabled policy: America's programs for the handicapped.* New York: Cambridge University Press.

Berkowitz, Edward D. 1991. *America's welfare state: From Roosevelt to Reagan.* Baltimore: Johns Hopkins University Press.

Berkowitz, Edward D. 1995. *Mr Social Security: The life of Wilbur J. Cohen.* Lawrence: University Press of Kansas.

Berkowitz, Edward D. 2003. *Robert Ball and the politics of Social Security.* Madison: University of Wisconsin Press.

Berkowitz, Edward D. 2006. *Something happened: A political and cultural overview of the seventies.* New York: Columbia University Press.

Bernstein, Irving. 1985. *A caring society: The New Deal, the worker, and the Great Depression.* Boston: Houghton Mifflin.

Bertozzi, Fabio, and Fabrizio Gilardi. 2008. "The Swiss welfare state: A changing public–private mix?" In Daniel Béland and Brian Gran, eds, *Public and private social policy: Health and pension policies in a new era,* 207–27. Basingstoke: Palgrave Macmillan.

Beveridge, William. 1942. *Social insurance and allied services.* New York: Macmillan.

Bhatia, Vandna, and William D. Coleman. 2003. "Ideas and discourse: Reform and resistance in the Canadian and German health systems." *Canadian Journal of Political Science* 36(4): 715–39.

Bianchi, Suzanne M. 1995. "Changing economic roles of women and men." In Reynolds Farley, ed., *State of the Union: America in the 1990s. Volume One: Economic trends,* 107–54. New York: Russell Sage Foundation.

Blackmore, Ken. 1998. *Social policy: An introduction.* Milton Keynes: Open University Press.

Blau, Francine D., and Lawrence M. Kahn. 2006. "The gender pay gap: Going,

going . . . but not gone." In Francine D. Blau, Marcy C. Brinton, and David B. Grusky, eds, *The declining significance of gender?*, 37–66. New York: Russell Sage Foundation.

Blau, Judith, and Keri E. Iyall Smith. 2006. *Public sociologies reader*. Boulder, CO: Rowman & Littlefield Publishers.

Blyth, Mark. 2002. *Great transformations: Economic ideas and institutional change in the twentieth century*. Cambridge: Cambridge University Press.

Bogenschneider, Karen. 2004. "Has family policy come of age? A decade review of the state of US family policy in the 1990s." *Journal of Marriage and Family* 62(4): 1136–59.

Bolduan, Kate. 2009. "The plight of young, uninsured Americans." *CNN*, March 7. http://www.cnn.com/2009/POLITICS/03/07/young.uninsured/index.html (accessed March 18, 2010).

Bonoli, Giuliano. 1997. "Classifying welfare states: A two-dimension approach." *Journal of Social Policy* 26(3): 351–72.

Bonoli, Giuliano. 2000. *The politics of pension reform: Institutions and policy change in Western Europe*. Cambridge: Cambridge University Press.

Bonoli, Giuliano. 2005. "The politics of the new social policies: Providing coverage against new social risks in mature welfare states." *Policy & Politics* 33(3): 431–49.

Bonoli, Giuliano. 2006. "New social risks and the politics of post-industrial social policies." In Klaus Armingeon and Giuliano Bonoli, eds, *The politics of post-industrial welfare states: Adapting post-war social policies to new social risks*, 3–26. London: Routledge.

Borjas, George J. 2006. "Wage trends among disadvantaged minorities." In Rebecca M. Blank, Sheldon H. Danziger, and Robert F. Schoeni, eds, *Working and poor: How economic and policy changes are affecting low-wage workers*, 59–86. New York: Russell Sage Foundation.

Boschee, Marlys Ann, and Geralyn M. Jacobs. 1997. "Childcare in the United States: Yesterday and today." Ames, IA: National Network for Child Care. http://www.nncc.org/Choose.Quality.Care/ccyesterd.html (accessed Maech 18, 2010).

Boychuk, Gerard W. 2006. "Slouching toward the bottom? Provincial social assistance provision in Canada, 1980–2000." In Kathryn Harrison, ed., *Racing to the bottom? Provincial interdependence in the Canadian federation*, 157–92. Vancouver: UBC Press.

Boychuk, Gerard W. 2008. *National health insurance in the United States and Canada: Race, territory, and the roots of difference*. Washington, DC: Georgetown University Press.

Boychuk, Gerard W., and Keith G. Banting. 2008. "The Canadian paradox: The public–private divide in health insurance and pensions." In Daniel Béland and Brian Gran, eds, *Public and private social policy: Health and pension policies in a new era*, 92–122. Basingstoke: Palgrave Macmillan.

Brandsen, Taco, and Jan-Kees Helderman. 2006. "The rewards of policy legacy: Why Dutch social housing did not follow the British path." In Liesbet Heyse, Sandra Resodihardjo, Tineke Lantink, and Berber Lettinga, eds, *Reform in Europe: Breaking the barriers in government*, 37–56. Aldershot: Ashgate.

Bremer, William W. 1975. "Along the way: The New Deal's work relief programs for the unemployed." *Journal of American History* 62(December): 636–52.

Brodie, Janine. 2002. "Citizenship and solidarity: Reflections on the Canadian way." *Citizenship Studies* 6: 377–94.

Brooks, Clem, and Jeff Manza. 2007. *Why welfare states persist: The importance of public opinion in democracies*. Chicago: University of Chicago Press.

Brooks, John Graham. 1893. *Compulsory insurance in Germany*. Washington, DC: United States Government Printing Office.

Brown, Drusilla K., Alan V. Deardorff, and Robert M. Stern. 1996. "International labor standards and trade: A theoretical analysis." In Jagdish Bhagwati and Robert Hudec, eds, *Harmonization and fair trade: Prerequisites for free trade?*, 227–80. Cambridge, MA: MIT Press.

Brown, Lawrence D., and Michael S. Sparer. 2003. "Poor program's progress: The unanticipated politics of Medicaid policy." *Health Affairs* 22(1): 31–44.

Brown, Michael K. 1999. *Race, money, and the American welfare state*. Ithaca, NY: Cornell University Press.

Brownlee, W. Elliot, and Hugh Davis Graham, eds. 2003. *The Reagan presidency: Pragmatic conservatism and its legacies*. Lawrence: University Press of Kansas.

Burawoy, Michael. 2005. "For public sociology." *American Sociological Review* 70(1): 4–28.

Campbell, Andrea Louise. 2003. *How policies make citizens: Senior citizen activism and the American welfare state*. Princeton: Princeton University Press.

Campbell, John L. 2002. "Ideas, politics, and public policy." *Annual Review of Sociology* 28: 21–38.

Campbell, John L. 2004. *Institutional change and globalization*. Princeton: Princeton University Press.

Campbell, John L., and Pedersen, Ove. K. 2010. "Knowledge regimes and the varieties of capitalism." In Daniel Béland and Robert H. Cox, eds, *Ideas and Politics in Social Science Research*. New York: Oxford University Press.

Campeau, Georges. 2005. *From UI to EI: Waging war on the welfare state*. Vancouver: UBC Press.

Cannon, Michael F. 2009. *Fannie Med? Why a "public option" is hazardous to your health*. Washington, DC: CATO Institute (Policy Analysis No. 642).

Castel, Robert. 2003. *From manual workers to wage laborers: Transformation of the social question*. New Brunswick, NJ: Transaction Publishers.

Castles, Francis G., ed. 1993. *Families of nations*. Dartmouth: Aldershot.

Castles, Francis G. 2004. *The future of the welfare state: crisis myths and crisis realities*. Oxford: Oxford University Press.

Castles, Francis G., and Deborah Mitchell. 1992. "Identifying welfare state regimes: The links between politics, instruments and outcomes." *Governance* 5(1): 1–26.

Cates, Jerry R. 1983. *Insuring inequality: Administrative leadership in Social Security, 1935–1954*. Ann Arbor: University of Michigan Press.

Cazenave, Noel A. 2007. *Impossible democracy: The unlikely success of the War on Poverty community action programs*. Albany: State University of New York Press.

Children's Defense Fund. *The state of America's children 2005*. Washington, DC: Children's Defense Fund.

Clark, Andrew. 2009. "Evil and Orwellian: America's right turns its fire on NHS." *Guardian*, August 12.

Clasen, Jochen and Nico A. Siegel (eds), *Investigating welfare state change: The "dependent variable problem" in comparative analysis*. Cheltenham: Edward Elgar.

Clawson, Dan, Robert Zussman, Joya Misra, Naomi Gerstel, Randall Stokes, Douglas J. Anderton, and Michael Burawoy. *Public sociology*. Berkeley: University of California Press.

CNN. 2010. "Obama signs health care 'fixes' bill," CNN, March 30. http://www.cnn.com/2010/POLITICS/03/30/pol.health.care/?hpt=Sbin (accessed April 7, 2010).

Cohen, Robin, and Paul Kennedy. 2000. *Global sociology*. Basingstoke: Palgrave Macmillan.

Congressional Budget Office. 2005. *Global population aging in the 21st century and its economic implications*. Washington, DC: Congressional Budget Office.

Conlan, Timothy J. 1998. *From new federalism to devolution: Twenty-five years of intergovernmental reform*. Washington, DC: Brookings Institution Press.

Cox, Robert H. 1998. "The consequences of welfare reform: How conceptions of social rights are changing." *Journal of Social Policy* 27(1): 1–16.

Cox, Robert H. 2001. "The social construction of an imperative: Why welfare reform happened in Denmark and the Netherlands but not in Germany." *World Politics* 53: 463–98.

Cox, Robert H. 2004. "The path dependence of an idea." *Social Policy & Administration* 38(2): 204–19.

Daguerre, Anne. 2004. "Importing workfare: Policy transfer of social and labour market policies from the USA to Britain under New Labour." *Social Policy & Administration* 38(1): 41–56.

Dalmia, Shikha. 2006. "Illegal immigrants are paying a lot more taxes than you think." *Knight Ridder/Tribune News Service*, May 1.

Davies, Gareth. 1996. *From opportunity to entitlement: The transformation and decline of great society liberalism*. Lawrence: University Press of Kansas.

Davies, Gareth, and Martha Derthick. 1997. "Race and social welfare policy: The Social Security Act of 1935." *Political Science Quarterly* 112(2): 217–36.

Deacon, Bob. 2007. *Global social policy and governance*. London: Sage.

References

Dean, Hartley. 2007. *Social policy*. Cambridge: Polity.

Derthick, Martha. 1979. *Policymaking for social security*. Washington, DC: Brookings Institution Press.

DeWitt, Larry. 1996. "Origins of the three-legged stool metaphor for social security." Baltimore: Social Security Administration (Historian's Office). http://www.ssa.gov/history/stool.html (accessed March 18, 2010).

DeWitt, Larry, Daniel Béland, and Edward D. Berkowitz. 2007. *Social Security: A documentary history*. Washington, DC: Congressional Quarterly Press.

Dicker, John. 2005. *The United States of Wal-Mart*. New York: Penguin.

Doling, John. 1997. *Comparative housing policy: Government and housing in advanced industrialized countries*. New York: St Martin's Press.

Dollar, David. 2007. "Globalization, poverty and inequality since 1980." In David Held and Ayse Kaya, eds, *Global inequality: Patterns and explanations*, 73–103. Cambridge: Polity.

Dwyer, Peter. 2004. "Creeping conditionality in the UK: From welfare rights to conditional entitlements?" *Canadian Journal of Sociology* 29(4): 265–87.

Ebbinghaus, Bernhard. 2006. *Reforming early retirement in Europe, Japan and the USA*. Oxford: Oxford University Press.

Edsall, Thomas. 1984. *The new politics of inequality*. New York: W. W. Norton.

Edwards, George C., III. 2007. *Governing by campaigning: The politics of the Bush presidency*. New York: Pearson Longman.

Eldersveld, Samuel J. 2007. *Poor America: A comparative historical study of poverty in the United States and Western Europe*. Lanham, MD: Lexington Books.

Erkulwater, Jennifer L. 2006. *Disability rights and the American social safety net*. Ithaca, NY: Cornell University Press.

Esping-Andersen, Gøsta. 1985. *Politics against markets: The social democratic road to power*. Princeton: Princeton University Press.

Esping-Andersen, Gøsta. 1990. *The three worlds of welfare capitalism*. Cambridge: Polity.

Esping-Andersen, Gøsta. 1996. "After the Golden Age? Welfare state dilemmas in a global economy." In Gøsta Esping-Andersen, ed., *Welfare states in transition*, 1–31. London: Sage.

Esping-Andersen, Gøsta. 1999. *Social foundations of postindustrial economies*. Oxford: Oxford University Press.

Esping-Andersen, Gøsta, with Duncan Gallie, Anton Hemerijck, and John Myles. 2002. *Why we need a new welfare state*. Oxford: Oxford University Press.

Evans, Eric J. 2004. *Thatcher and Thatcherism* (Second Edition). London: Routledge.

Ewald, François. 1986. *L'État-providence*. Paris: Grasset.

Ferrera, Maurizio. 1996. "The southern model of welfare in social Europe." *Journal of European Social Policy* 6(1): 17–37.

Fine, Sidney. 1956. *Laissez faire and the general-welfare state: A study of conflict in American thought, 1865–1901*. Ann Arbor: University of Michigan Press.

Finegold, Kenneth. 2005. "The United States: Federalism and its counter-factuals." In Herbert Obinger, Stephan Leibfried, and Francis G. Castles, eds, *Federalism and the welfare state*, 138–78. Cambridge: Cambridge University Press.

Fite, Gilbert C., and Jim E. Reese. 1973. *An economic history of the United States* (Third Edition). Boston: Houghton Mifflin Company.

Flora, Peter, and Heidenheimer, Arnold J. 1981. "The historical core and changing boundaries of the welfare state." In Peter Flora and Arnold J. Heidenheimer, eds, *The development of welfare states in Europe and America*, 17–34. New Brunswick, NJ: Transaction Books.

Forbath, William E. 1991. *Law and the shaping of the American labor movement.* Cambridge: MA: Harvard University Press.

Fox Piven, Frances, and Richard Cloward. 1971. *Regulating the poor: The functions of public welfare.* New York: Pantheon Books.

Franklin, William. 1898. *Workingmen's insurance.* New York: Thomas Y. Crowell.

Fraser, Nancy, and Linda Gordon. 1992. "Contract versus charity: Why is there no social citizenship in the United States?" *Socialist Review* 22(July): 45–68.

Fraser, Nancy, and Linda Gordon. 1994. "'Dependency' demystified: Inscriptions of power in a keyword of the welfare state." *Social Politics* 1(1): 4–31.

Galenson, Walter. 1996. *The American labor movement, 1955–1995.* Westport, CT: Greenwood Press.

Garner, Roberta, ed. 2000. *Social theory: Continuity and confrontation.* Peterborough: Broadview Press.

Gavrilov, Leonid A., and Patrick Heuveline. 2003. "Aging of population." In Paul Demeny and Geoffrey McNicoll, eds, *The encyclopedia of population*, Vol. 1, 32–7. New York: Macmillan.

Genschel, Philipp. 2004. "Globalization and the welfare state: A retrospective." *Journal of European Public Policy* 11(4): 613–36.

Ghilarducci, Teresa. 2008. *When I'm sixty-four: The plot against pensions and the plan to save them.* Princeton: Princeton University Press.

Giddens, Anthony. 1990. *The consequences of modernity.* Cambridge: Polity.

Giddens, Anthony. 1994. *Beyond left and right: The future of radical politics.* Cambridge: Polity.

Giddens, Anthony. 1998. *The third way: The renewal of social democracy.* Cambridge: Polity.

Gifford, Brian. 2006. "The camouflaged safety net: The U.S. armed forces as welfare state institution." *Social Politics* 13(3): 372–99.

Gilbert, Neil. 2002. *Transformation of the welfare state.* New York: Oxford University Press.

Glaeser, Edward L., and Jesse M. Shapiro. 2002. *The benefits of the home mortgage interest deduction.* Discussion Paper Number 1979 (October). Cambridge, MA: Harvard Institute of Economic Research.

References

Glennerster, Howard. 2000. *British social policy since 1945* (Second Edition). Oxford: Blackwell.

Gordon, Colin. 1997. "Why no health insurance in the US? The limits of social provision in war and peace, 1941–1948." *Journal of Policy History* 9(3): 277–310.

Gordon, Linda. 1994. *Pitied but not entitled: Single mothers and the history of welfare.* New York: Free Press.

Gornick, Janet C., and Marcia Meyers. 2003. *Families that work: Policies for reconciling parenthood and employment.* New York: Russell Sage Foundation.

Graebner, William. 1980. *A history of retirement: The function of an American institution.* New Haven: Yale University Press.

Gran, Brian. 2003. "A second opinion: Rethinking the public–private dichotomy for health insurance." *International Journal of Health Services* 33(2): 283–313.

Gran, Brian, and Daniel Béland. 2008. "Conclusion: Revisiting the public–private dichotomy." In Daniel Béland and Brian Gran, eds, *Public and private social policy: Health and pension policies in a new era,* 269–81. Basingstoke: Palgrave Macmillan.

Guillén, Mauro F. 2001. "Is globalization civilizing, destructive or feeble? A critique of six key debates in the social science literature." *Annual Review of Sociology* 27: 235–60.

Haas, Linda. 2004. "Parental leave and gender equality: What can the United States learn from the European Union?" In Heidi Gottfried and Laura Ann Reese, eds, *Equity in the workplace: Gendering workplace policy analysis,* 183–214. Lanham, MD: Lexington Books.

Hacker, Jacob S. 1997. *The road to nowhere: The genesis of President Clinton's plan for health security.* Princeton: Princeton University Press.

Hacker, Jacob S. 2002. *The divided welfare state: The battle over public and private social benefits in the United States.* Cambridge: Cambridge University Press.

Hacker, Jacob S. 2004. "Privatizing risk without privatizing the welfare state: The hidden politics of social policy retrenchment in the United States." *American Political Science Review* 98(2): 243–60.

Hacker, Jacob S. 2006. *The great risk shift.* New York: Oxford University Press.

Hacker, Jacob S. 2008. *The case for public plan choice in national health reform: Key to cost control and quality coverage.* Washington, DC: Institute for America's Future.

Hacker, Jacob S., and Paul Pierson. 2002. "Business power and social policy: Employers and the formation of the American welfare state." *Politics and Society* 30(2): 277–325.

Hacker, Jacob S., and Paul Pierson. 2005. *Off center: The Republican revolution and the erosion of American democracy.* New Haven: Yale University Press.

Hale, Geoffrey E. 1998. "Reforming employment insurance: Transcending the politics of the status quo." *Canadian Public Policy* 24(4): 429–51.

References

Hall, John A., and John Ikenberry. 1989. *The state*. Minneapolis: University of Minnesota Press.

Hall, Peter A. 1993. "Policy paradigms, social learning and the state: The case of economic policymaking in Britain." *Comparative Politics* 25(3): 275–96.

Hall, Stuart, and Martin Jacques, eds. 1983. *The politics of Thatcherism*. London: Lawrence and Wishart.

Hansen, Randall, and Desmond King. 2001. "Eugenic ideas, political interests, and policy variance: Immigration and sterilization policy in Britain and the US." *World Politics* 53: 237–63.

Harden, Blaine. 2009. "Japan works hard to help immigrants find jobs: Population-loss fears prompt new stance." *Washington Post*, January 23: A01.

Harrington, Michael. 1962. *The other America: Poverty in the United States*. New York: Macmillan.

Hattam, Victoria C. 1993. *Labor visions and state power: The origins of business unionism in the United States*. Princeton: Princeton University Press.

Hartz, Louis. 1955. *The liberal tradition in America: An interpretation of American political thought since the revolution*. New York: Harcourt Brace & World.

Hayek, F.A. 2007. *The road to serfdom: Text and documents – the definitive edition*. Chicago: University of Chicago Press.

Head Start Impact Study. 2005. *Head Start Impact Study: First year findings. Executive summary*. Washington, DC: US Department of Health and Human Services.

Heclo, Hugh. 1974. *Modern social politics in Britain and Sweden: From relief to income maintenance*. New Haven: Yale University Press.

Hicks, Alexander. 1999. *Social democracy and welfare capitalism: A century of income security politics*. Ithaca, NY: Cornell University Press.

Hill, Michael. 2003. *Understanding social policy* (Seventh Edition). Oxford: Blackwell.

Hinrichs, Karl, and Olli Kangas. 2003. "When is a change big enough to be a system shift? Small system-shifting changes in German and Finnish pension policies." *Social Policy & Administration* 37(6): 573–91.

Howard, Christopher. 1997. *The hidden welfare state: Tax expenditures and social policy in the United States*. Princeton: Princeton University Press.

Howard, Christopher. 2006. *The welfare state nobody knows: Debunking myths about US social policy*. Princeton: Princeton University Press.

Howard, Christopher, and Edward D. Berkowitz. 2008. "Extensive but not inclusive: Health care and pensions in the United States." In Daniel Béland and Brian Gran, eds, *Public and private social policy: Health and pension policies in a new era*, 70–91. Basingstoke: Palgrave Macmillan.

Huang, Chye-Ching, and Hannah Shaw. 2009. *New analysis shows "tax expenditures" overall are costly and regressive*. Washington, DC: Center on Budget and Policy Priorities.

Huber, Evelyne, and John D. Stephens. 2001. *Development and crisis of the welfare state: Parties and policies in global markets.* Chicago: University of Chicago Press.

Huber, Evelyne, and John D. Stephens. 2006. "Combating old and new social risks." In Klaus Armingeon and Giuliano Bonoli, eds, *The politics of post-industrial welfare states: Adapting post-war social policies to new social risks,* 143–68. London: Routledge.

Hunt, Kelly A., and James R. Knickman. 2008. "Financing health care." In Anthony R. Kovner and Steven Jonas, eds, *Jonas & Kovner's health care delivery in the United States,* 46–89. New York: Springer.

Immergut, Ellen L. 1992. *Health politics: Interest and institutions in Western Europe.* Cambridge: Cambridge University Press.

Iversen, Torben. 2005. *Capitalism, democracy, and welfare.* New York: Cambridge University Press.

Jacobs, Alan M. 2008. "The politics of when: Redistribution, investment, and the politics of the long term." *British Journal of Political Science* 38(2): 193–220.

Jacobs, Alan M., and Steven M. Teles. 2007. "The perils of market making: The case of British pension reform." In Marc Landy, Martin Levin, and Martin Shapiro, eds, *Creating competitive markets,* 157–83. Washington, DC: Brookings Institution Press.

Jaeger, Paul T., and Cynthia Ann Bowman. 2005. *Understanding disability: Inclusion, access, diversity, and civil rights.* Westport, CT: Greenwood Press.

Jaenicke, Douglas, and Alex Waddan. 2006. "President Bush and social policy: The strange case of the Medicare prescription drug benefit." *Political Science Quarterly* 121(2): 217–40.

Jansson, Bruce S. 2009. *The reluctant welfare state* (Sixth Edition). Belmont, CA: Brooks/Cole.

Jenson, Jane. 2004. *Canada's new social risks: Directions for a new social architecture.* Ottawa: Canadian Policy Research Networks.

Jenson, Jane, and Denis Saint-Martin. 2006. "Building blocks for a new social architecture: The LEGO™ paradigm of an active society." *Policy & Politics* 34(3): 429–51.

Johnson, Hans P., and Margaret O'Brien-Strain. 2000. *Getting to know the future customers of the Office of Child Support: Projections Report for 2004 and 2009.* Washington, DC: The Office of Child Support Enforcement.

Johnson, Paul, and Sarah Tanner. 1998. "Ownership and the distribution of wealth." *Political Quarterly* 69(4): 365–74.

Jones, Catherine. 1993. "The Pacific challenge: Confucian welfare states." In Catherine Jones, ed., *New perspectives on the welfare state in Europe,* 198–217. London: Routledge.

Kaiser Family Foundation. 2010. *Side-by-side comparison of major health care reform proposals.* Washington, DC: Kaiser Family Foundation.

Kamerman, Sheila, and Shirley Gatenio. 2002. "Mother's Day: More than candy and flowers, working parents need paid time-off." New York: The Clearinghouse on International Developments in Child, Youth & Family Policies (Columbia University). http://www.childpolicyintl.org/issuebrief/issuebrief5.htm (accessed March 18, 2010).

Kasza, Gregory J. 2002. "The illusion of welfare 'regimes'." *Journal of Social Policy* 31(2): 271–97.

Katz, Michael B. 1996. *In the shadow of the poorhouse* (Second Edition). New York: Basic Books.

Katz, Michael B. 2008. *The price of citizenship: Redefining the American welfare state* (Second Edition). Philadelphia: University of Pennsylvania Press.

Katznelson, Ira. 2005. *When affirmative action was white: An untold history of racial inequality in twentieth-century America.* New York: W. W. Norton & Company.

Kay, Stephen J. 1999. "Unexpected privatizations: Politics and social security reform in the Southern Cone." *Comparative Politics* 31(4): 403–22.

Kengor, Paul, and Peter Schweizer, eds. 2005. *The Reagan presidency: Assessing the man and his legacy.* Boulder, CO: Rowman & Littlefield.

Kerr, Clark, John T. Dunlop, Frederick Harbison, and Charles A. Myers. 1964. *Industrialism and industrial man: The problems of labor and management in economic growth* (Second Edition). Oxford: Oxford University Press.

Kessler-Harris, Alice. 2001. *In pursuit of equity: Women, men, and the quest for economic citizenship in 20th-century America.* New York: Oxford University Press.

King, Desmond, and Mark Wickham-Jones. 1999. "From Clinton to Blair: The Democratic (Party) origins of welfare to work." *Political Quarterly* 70 (1): 62–74.

King, Leslie. 1998. "'France needs children': Pronatalism, nationalism and women's equity." *The Sociological Quarterly* 39(1): 33–52.

King, Ronald F. 2000. *Budgeting entitlements: The politics of food stamps.* Washington, DC: Georgetown University Press.

Klein, Jennifer. 2003. *For all these rights: Business, labor, and the shaping of America's public–private welfare state.* Princeton: Princeton University Press.

Korpi, Walter. 1983. *The democratic class struggle.* Boston: Routledge and Kegan Paul.

Korpi, Walter. 2003. "Welfare state regress in Western Europe." *Annual Review of Sociology* 29: 589–609.

Kpessa, Michael. 2009. *Resistance, continuity, and change: The politics of pension reforms in English-speaking Sub-Saharan Africa.* Hamilton: McMaster University (Ph.D. dissertation in political science).

Kymlicka, Will. 2005. "The uncertain futures of multiculturalism." *Canadian Diversity* 4(1): 82–5.

Kymlicka, Will, and Wayne Norman. 1995. "Return of the citizen: A survey of recent work on citizenship theory." In Ronald Beiner, ed., *Theorizing citizenship*, 283–322. Albany: State University of New York Press.

References

Lancaster, Carol. 2006. *Foreign aid: Diplomacy, development, domestic politics.* Chicago: University of Chicago Press.

Laurin, Alexandre. 2006. *International tax burdens: Single individuals with or without children.* Ottawa: Library of Parliament (Government of Canada).

Leimgruber, Matthieu. 2008. *Solidarity without the state? Business and the shaping of the Swiss welfare state, 1890–2000.* Cambridge: Cambridge University Press.

Letwin, Shirley Robin. 1993. *The anatomy of Thatcherism.* New Brunswick, NJ: Transaction Publishers.

Levine, Daniel. 1988. *Poverty and society: The growth of the American welfare state in international comparison.* New Brunswick, NJ: Rutgers University Press.

Lewis, Jane. 1992. "Gender and the development of welfare regimes." *Journal of European Social Policy* 2: 159–73.

Lieberman, Robert C. 1998. *Shifting the color line: Race and the American welfare state.* Cambridge, MA: Harvard University Press.

Lieberman, Robert C. 2005. *Shaping race policy: The United States in comparative perspective.* Princeton: Princeton University Press.

Light, Paul C. 1995. *Still artful work: The continuing politics of Social Security reform.* New York: McGraw-Hill.

Lipset, Seymour Martin. 1990. *Continental divide: The values and institutions of the United States and Canada.* New York: Routledge.

Little, Bruce. 2008. *Fixing the future: How Canada's usually fractious governments worked together to rescue the Canada Pension Plan.* Toronto: University of Toronto Press.

Lovell, Vicky, Elizabeth O'Neill, and Skylar Olsen. 2007. *Maternity leave in the United States: Paid parental leave is still not standard, even among the best US employers.* Washington, DC: Institute for Women's Policy Research.

Lowi, Theodore. 1964. "American business and public policy: Case studies and political theory." *World Politics* 16(July): 677–715.

Lowi, Theodore 1984. "Why is there no socialism in the United States? A federal analysis." *International Political Science Review* 5(4): 369–80.

Lubove, Roy. 1968. *The struggle for social security, 1900–1935.* Cambridge, MA: Harvard University Press.

McClellan, Mark B., and Daniel P. Kessler, eds. 2002. *Technological change in health care: A global analysis of heart attack.* Ann Arbor: University of Michigan Press.

McElvaine, Robert S. 1984. *The Great Depression: America, 1929–1941.* New York: Times Books.

McEwen, Nicola. 2006. *Nationalism and the state: Welfare and identity in Scotland and Quebec.* Brussels: Peter Lang.

McLanahan, Sara, and Lynne Casper. 1995. "Growing diversity and inequality in the American family." In Reynolds Farley, ed., *State of the Union: America in the 1990s. Volume Two: Social trends*, 1–46. New York: Russell Sage Foundation.

Mahon, Rianne. 2001. "Theorizing welfare regimes: Toward a dialogue?" *Social Politics* 8(1): 24–35.

Maioni, Antonia. 1998. *Parting at the crossroads: The emergence of health insurance in the United States and Canada.* Princeton: Princeton University Press.

Malkin, Elisabeth. 2008. "Re-examining Nafta in hopes of curing US manufacturing." *New York Times*, April 22.

Marier, Patrik. 2005. "Where did the bureaucrats go? Role and influence of the public bureaucracy in the Swedish and French pension reform debate." *Governance* 18(4): 521–544.

Marier, Patrik. 2008. *Pension politics: Consensus and social conflict in ageing societies.* London: Routledge.

Marmor, Theodore R. 2000. *The politics of Medicare.* New York: Aldine de Gruyter.

Marmor, Theodore R., and Jerry L. Mashaw. 2006. "Understanding social insurance: Fairness, affordability, and the 'modernization' of Social Security and Medicare." *Health Affairs* 25(3): w114–34.

Marshall, T. H. 1964. "Citizenship and social class." In *Class, citizenship and development*, 65–122. Garden City, NY: Doubleday.

Martin, Isaac. 2008. *The permanent tax revolt: How the property tax transformed American politics.* Palo Alto, CA: Stanford University Press.

Massey, Douglas S. 2007. *Categorically unequal: The American stratification system.* New York: Russell Sage Foundation.

Mayes, Rick. 2004. *Universal coverage: The elusive quest for national health insurance.* Ann Arbor: University of Michigan Press.

Mayhew, David R. 1974. *Congress: The electoral connection.* New Haven: Yale University Press.

Merrien, François-Xavier. 1997. *L'État-providence.* Paris: Presses Universitaires de France.

Mettler, Suzanne. 1998. *Dividing citizens: Gender and federalism in New Deal public policy.* Ithaca, NY: Cornell University Press.

Mettler, Suzanne. 2005. *Soldiers to citizens: The GI Bill and the making of the greatest generation.* New York: Oxford University Press.

Milanovic, Branko. 2005. *Worlds apart: Measuring international and global inequality.* Princeton: Princeton University Press.

Milanovic, Barnko. 2006. "Global income inequality: What it is and why it matters." Department of Economics and Social Affairs Working Paper No. 26. New York: United Nations. http://www.un.org/esa/desa/papers/2006/wp26_2006.pdf (accessed March 18, 2010).

Mishra, Ramesh. 1999. *Globalization and the welfare state.* Cheltenham: Edward Elgar.

Morgan, Kimberly J. 2006. *Working mothers and the welfare state: Religion and the politics of work–family policies in Western Europe and the United States.* Stanford: Stanford University Press.

Moss, David A. 1995. *Socializing security: Progressive-Era economists and the origins of American social policy.* Cambridge, MA: Harvard University Press.

Moss, David A. 2002. *When all else fails: Government as the ultimate risk manager.* Cambridge, MA: Harvard University Press.

Moynihan, Daniel Patrick. 1969. *Maximum feasible misunderstanding: Community action in the War on Poverty.* New York: Free Press.

Murray, Charles. 1994. *Losing ground: American social policy, 1950–1980* (Tenth Anniversary Edition). New York: Free Press.

Myles, John. 1988. "Postwar capitalism and the extension of social security into a retirement wage." In Margaret Weir, Ann Shola Orloff, and Theda Skocpol, eds, *The politics of social policy in the United States*, 265–84. Princeton: Princeton University Press.

Myles, John. 1989. *Old age in the welfare state: The political economy of public pensions* (Second Edition). Lawrence: University Press of Kansas.

Myles, John. 1997. "Neither rights nor contacts: The new means testing in US aging policy." In Robert B. Hudson, ed., *The future of age-based policy*, 46–55. Baltimore: Johns Hopkins University Press.Myles, John, and Paul Pierson. 1997. "Friedman's revenge: The reform of liberal welfare states in Canada and the United States." *Politics and Society* 25(4): 443–72.

Myles, John, and Paul Pierson. 2001. "The comparative political economy of pension reform." In Paul Pierson, ed., *The new politics of the welfare state*, 305–33. Oxford: Oxford University Press.

Myles, John, and Jill Quadagno. 2002. "Political theories of the welfare state." *Social Service Review* 76(1): 34–57.

Nash, George H. 1996. *The conservative intellectual movement in America since 1945* (Second Edition). Wilmington, DE: Intercollegiate Studies Institute.

Nelson, Daniel. 1969. *Unemployment insurance: The American experience, 1915–1935.* Madison: University of Wisconsin Press.

Nichols, Lawrence T., ed. 2007. *Public sociology: The contemporary debate.* New Brunswick, NJ: Transaction Publishers.

Noël, Alain. 1999. "Is decentralization conservative? Federalism and the contemporary debate on the Canadian welfare state." In Robert Young, ed., *Stretching the federation: The art of the state in Canada*, 195–219. Kingston: Queen's Institute of Intergovernmental Relations.

Noël, Alain, and Jean-Philippe Thérien. 1995. "From domestic to international justice: The welfare state and foreign aid." *International Organization* 49(3): 523–53.

Numbers, Ronald L. 1978. *Almost persuaded: American physicians and compulsory health insurance, 1912–1920.* Baltimore: Johns Hopkins University Press.

Obama, Barack. 2009. "Remarks by the President to a joint session of Congress on health care." Washington, DC: The White House (Office of the Press Secretary), September 9.

Obama, Barack. 2010. "Remarks by the President in State of the Union Address." Washington, DC: The White House (Office of the Press Secretary), January 27.

Oberlander, Jonathan. 2003. *The political life of Medicare.* Chicago: University of Chicago Press.

Obinger, Herbert, Stephan Leibfried, and Francis G. Castles. 2005a. "Introduction: Federalism and the welfare state." In Herbert Obinger, Stephan Leibfried, and Francis G. Castles, eds, *Federalism and the welfare state: New World and European experiences,* 1–48. Cambridge: Cambridge University Press.

Obinger, Herbert, Stephan Leibfried, and Francis G. Castles, eds. 2005b. *Federalism and the welfare state: New World and European experiences.* Cambridge: Cambridge University Press.

O'Connor, James. 1973. *Fiscal crisis of the state.* New York: St Martin's Press.

O'Connor, Julia S. 2002. "Understanding the welfare state and welfare states: Theoretical perspectives." In Douglas Bear, ed., *Political sociology: Canadian perspectives,* 110–28. Oxford: Oxford University Press.

O'Connor, Julia S., Ann Shola Orloff, and Sheila Shaver. 1999. *States, markets, families: Gender, liberalism and social policy in Australia, Canada, Great Britain and the United States.* Cambridge: Cambridge University Press.

Offe, Claus. 1982. "Some contradictions of the modern welfare state." *Critical Social Policy* 2(5): 7–16

Offe, Claus. 1984. *Contradictions of the welfare state.* Cambridge, MA: MIT Press.

Olsen, Gregg M. 2002. *The politics of the welfare state: Canada, Sweden, and the United States.* Toronto: Oxford University Press.

Olssen, Mark, John A. Codd, and Anne-Marie O'Neill. 2004. *Education policy: Globalization, citizenship and democracy.* London: Sage.

Orenstein, Mitchell A. 2008. *Privatizing pensions: The transnational campaign for social security reform.* Princeton: Princeton University Press.

Orloff, Ann Shola. 1993a. *The politics of pensions: A comparative analysis of Britain, Canada, and the United States, 1880–1940.* Madison: University of Wisconsin Press.

Orloff, Ann Shola. 1993b. "Gender and the social rights of citizenship: The comparative analysis of gender relations and welfare states." *American Sociological Review* 58: 303–28.

Orloff, Ann Shola, and Bruno Palier, eds. 2009. "Special Issue: The power of gender perspectives: Feminist influence on policy paradigms, social science and social politics." *Social Politics* 16(4).

Orren, Karen, and Stephen Skowronek. 2004. *The search for American political development.* New York: Cambridge University Press.

Padamsee, Tasleem. 2007. *Infusing health into the welfare state: HIV/AIDS policy making in the United States and the United Kingdom.* University of Michigan: Ph.D. dissertation (sociology).

References

Padamsee, Tasleem. 2009. "Culture in connection: Re-contextualizing ideational processes in the analysis of policy development." *Social Politics* 16(4): 413–45.

Palier, Bruno. 2002. *Gouverner la sécurité sociale*. Paris: Presses Universitaires de France.

Palier, Bruno. 2006. "Beyond retrenchment: Four problems in current welfare state research and one suggestion on how to overcome them." In Christopher Pierson and Francis G. Castles, eds, *The welfare state reader* (Second Edition), 358–74. Cambridge: Policy Press.

Papillon, Martin, and Gina Cosentino. 2004. *Lessons from abroad: Towards a new social model for Canada's aboriginal peoples*. Ottawa: Canadian Policy Research Networks CPRN Social Architecture Papers: Research Report F|40.

Parsons, Craig. 2002. "Showing ideas as causes: The origins of the European Union." *International Organization* 56(1): 47–84.

Parsons, Craig. 2007. *How to map arguments in political science*. Oxford: Oxford University Press.

Petersen, Jørn Henrik, and Klaus Petersen. 2009. "On the origins of the term 'welfare state' in Germany and Britain." Unpublished paper. Odense: University of Southern Denmark.

Peterson, Paul E. 1995. *The price of federalism*. Washington, DC: Brookings Institution Press.

Pfau-Effinger, Birgit. 2005. "Culture and welfare state policies: Reflections on a complex interrelation." *Journal of Social Policy* 34(1): 3–20.

Pickering, Kathleen, Mark H. Harvey, Gene F. Summers, and David Mushinksi. 2006. *Welfare reform in persistent rural poverty: Dreams, disenchantments, and diversity*. University Park: Penn State University Press.

Pierson, Christopher, and Francis G. Castles, eds, 2006. *The welfare state reader*. Cambridge: Polity.

Pierson, Paul. 1994. *Dismantling the welfare state? Reagan, Thatcher, and the politics of retrenchment*. New York: Cambridge University Press.

Pierson, Paul. 1996. "The new politics of the welfare state." *World Politics* 48(1): 143–79.

Pierson, Paul, ed. 2001. *The new politics of the welfare state*. Oxford: Oxford University Press.

Pierson, Paul. 2004. *Politics in time: History, institutions, and social analysis*. Princeton: Princeton University Press.

Pimpare, Stephen. 2004. *The new Victorians: Poverty, politics, and propaganda in two gilded ages*. New York: New Press.

Piven, Frances Fox, and Richard Cloward. 1971. *Regulating the poor: The functions of public welfare*. New York: Pantheon.

Polakow, Valerie, and Cindy Guillean, eds. 2001. *International perspectives on homelessness*. Westport, CT: Greenwood Press.

Polanyi, Karl. 2001. *The great transformation: The political and economic origins of our time*. Boston: Beacon Press.

References

Popkin, Susan J., Victoria E. Gwiasda, Lynn M. Olson, Dennis P. Rosenbaum, and Larry Buron. 2000. *The hidden war: Crime and the tragedy of public housing in Chicago.* New Brunswick, NJ: Rutgers University Press.

Popple, Philip R., and Leslie Neighninger. 2003. *The policy-based profession: An introduction to social welfare policy analysis for social workers.* Boston: Allyn & Bacon.

Pratico, Dominick. 2001. *Eisenhower and Social Security: The origins of the Disability Program.* New York: Writers Club Press.

Pratt, Henry J. 1993. *Gray agendas: Interest groups and the public pensions in Canada, Britain, and the United States.* Ann Arbor: University of Michigan Press.

Quadagno, Jill. 1988. *The transformation of old age security: Class and politics in the American welfare state.* Chicago: University of Chicago Press.

Quadagno, Jill. 1994. *The color of welfare: How racism undermined the War on Poverty.* Oxford: Oxford University Press.

Quadagno, Jill. 2005. *One nation, uninsured: Why the US has no national health insurance.* New York: Oxford University Press.

Quadagno, Jill, and Debra Street. 2006. "Recent trends in US social welfare policy: Minor retrenchment or major transformation?" *Research on Aging* 28(3): 303–16.

Rawls, John. 1971. *A theory of justice.* Cambridge, MA: Belknap Press (Harvard University Press).

Reagan, Ronald. 1981. "Inaugural address." Washington, DC, January 20.

Rein, Martin, and Lee Rainwater, eds 1986. *Public/private interplay in social protection.* Armonk, NY: M. E. Sharpe.

Rein, Martin, and Winfried Schmähl, eds 2004. *Rethinking the welfare state: The political economy of pension reform.* London: Edward Elgar.

Reinhardt, Uwe E., Peter S. Hussey, and Gerard F. Anderson. 2004. "US health care spending in an international context: Why is US spending so high, and can we afford it?" *Health Affairs* 23(3): 10–25.

Rice, James J., and Michael J. Prince. 2000. *Changing politics of Canadian social policy.* Toronto: University of Toronto Press.

Rich, Andrew. 2004. *Think tanks, public policy, and the politics of expertise.* Cambridge: Cambridge University Press.

Rimlinger, Gaston. 1971. *Welfare policy and industrialization in America, Germany and Russia.* New York: Wiley.

Rodgers, Daniel T. 2000. *Atlantic crossings: Social politics in a progressive age.* Cambridge, MA: Harvard University Press.

Rodgers, Harrell R. 2006. *American poverty in a new era of reform* (Second Edition). Armonk, NY: M. E. Sharpe.

Rosanvallon, Pierre. 2000. *The new social question: Rethinking the welfare state.* Princeton: Princeton University Press.

Rosanvallon, Pierre. 1990. *L'État en France.* Paris: Le Seuil.

179

References

Rosner, Peter G. 2003. *The economics of social policy.* Cheltenham: Edward Elgar.

Rostow, Walt W. 1990. *The stages of economic growth: A non-communist manifesto.* Cambridge: Cambridge University Press.

Rothenberg, Paula S. 2006. *Race, class, and gender in the United States: An integrated study.* New York: Worth Publishers.

Rubinow, Isaac M. 1913. *Social insurance: With special reference to American conditions.* New York: Henry Holt and Company.

Ruggie, Mary. 1996. *Realignments in the welfare state: Health policy in the United States, Britain, and Canada.* New York: Columbia University Press.

Sainsbury, Diane. 1999. *Gender and welfare states regimes.* Oxford: Oxford University Press.

Saunders, Peter R., and Colin Harris. 1994. *Privatization and popular capitalism.* Milton Keynes: Open University Press.

Schickler, Eric. 2001. *Disjointed pluralism: Institutional innovation and the development of the US Congress.* Princeton: Princeton University Press.

Schieber, Sylvester J., and John B. Shoven. 1999. *The real deal: The history and future of social security.* New Haven: Yale University Press.

Schmidt, Vivien A. 2002. "Does discourse matter in the politics of welfare state adjustment?" *Comparative Political Studies* 35(2): 168–93.

Schmidt, Vivien A. 2010. "Reconciling ideas and institutions through discursive institutionalism" in Daniel Béland and Robert H. Cox, eds, *Ideas and politics in social science research.* New York: Oxford University Press.

Scholte, Jan Aart. 2002. *What is globalization? The definitional issue – again.* Coventry: University of Warwick, Centre for the Study of Globalization and Regionalization.

Schram, Sanford, Joe Soss, and Richard C. Fording, eds. 2003. *Race and the politics of welfare reform.* Ann Arbor: University of Michigan Press.

Schrecker, Ellen. 1998. *Many are the crimes: McCarthyism in America.* Princeton: Princeton University Press.

Schuck, Peter H. 2001. "Immigration reform redux." In Martin A. Levin, Marc Karnis Landy, and Martin M. Shapiro, eds, *Seeking the center: Politics and policymaking at the new century*, 113–31. Washington, DC: Georgetown University Press.

Schulman, Karen, and Helen Blank. 2008. *State child care assistance policies 2008: Too little progress for children and families.* Washington, DC: National Women's Law Center.

Seager, Henry L. 1910. *Social insurance.* New York: Macmillan.

Seeleib-Kaiser, Martin, ed. 2008. *Welfare state transformations.* Basingstoke: Palgrave Macmillan.

Seifert, Robert W. 2005. *Home sick: How medical debt undermines housing security.* Boston: The Access Project.

Sengupta, Ishita, Virginia Reno, and John F. Burton. 2007. *Workers' compensation: Benefits, coverage, and costs, 2005.* Washington, DC: National Academy of Social Insurance.

Shalev, Michael, ed. 1996. *The privatization of social policy? Occupational welfare and the welfare state in America, Scandinavia and Japan.* London: Macmillan.

Sherman, Emily. 2008. "Candidates ignoring coming social security crisis, critics say." *CNN*, October 23. http://www.cnn.com/2008/POLITICS/10/23/social.security/index.html (accessed March 18, 2010).

Shinkawa, Toshimitsu. 2008. "The Japanese familial welfare mix at a crossroads." In Daniel Béland and Brian Gran, eds, *Public and private social policy: Health and pension policies in a new era*, 228–48. Basingstoke: Palgrave Macmillan.

Skocpol, Theda. 1990. "Sustainable social policy: Fighting poverty without poverty programs." *The American Prospect* 1(2): 58–70.

Skocpol, Theda. 1992. *Protecting soldiers and mothers: The political origins of social policy in the United States.* Cambridge, MA: Belknap Press.

Skocpol, Theda. 1995. *Social policy in the United States: Future possibilities in historical perspective.* Princeton: Princeton University Press.

Skocpol, Theda, and Edwin Amenta. 1988. "Redefining the New Deal: World War II and the development of social policy in the United States." In Margaret Weir, Ann Schola Orloff, and Theda Skocpol, eds, *The politics of social policy in the United States*, 81–122. Princeton: Princeton University Press.

Smith, Peter C. and Witter, Sophie N. 2004. *Risk pooling in health care financing: the implications for health system performance.* Washington, DC: The World Bank (HNP Discussion Paper).

Smith Barusch, Amanda. 2008. *Foundations of social policy: social justice in human perspective* (Third Edition). Belmont, CA: Brooks/Cole.

Social Security Administration. 2008. *Annual report of the Supplemental Security Income Program.* Baltimore: Social Security Administration.

Sombart, Werner. 1976. *Why is there no socialism in the United States?* New York: M. E. Sharpe.

Somers, Margaret, and Block, Fred. 2005. "From poverty to perversity: Ideas, markets, and institutions over 200 years of welfare debate." *American Sociological Review* 70(2): 260–87.

Starr, Susan Sered, and Rushika Fernandopulle. 2005. *Uninsured in America: Life and death in the land of opportunity.* Berkeley: University of California Press.

Stateman, Alison. 2008. "Violence against the homeless: Is it a hate crime?" *Time Magazine*, October 22. http://www.time.com/time/nation/article/0,8599,1852825,00.html (accessed March 18, 2010).

Steensland, Brian. 2007. *The failed welfare revolution: America's struggle over guaranteed income policy.* Princeton: Princeton University Press.

Steinmo, Sven, and Jon Watts (1995), "It's the institutions, stupid! Why comprehensive national health insurance always fails in America," *Journal of Health Politics, Policy and Law* 20(2): 329–72.

References

Stephens, John D. 1979. *The transition from capitalism to socialism*. London: Macmillan.

Stevens, Beth. 1988. "Blurring the boundaries: How the federal government has influenced welfare benefits in the private sector." In Margaret Weir, Ann Schola Orloff, and Theda Skocpol, eds, *The politics of social policy in the United States*, 123–48. Princeton: Princeton University Press.

Stone, Diane. 2008. "Global public policy, transnational policy communities, and their networks." *Policy Studies Journal* 36(1): 19–38.

Streeck, Wolfgang, and Kathleen Thelen, eds 2005. *Beyond continuity: Institutional change in advanced political economies*. Oxford: Oxford University Press.

Street, Debra. 2008. "Balancing acts: Trends in the public–private mix in health care." In Daniel Béland and Brian Gran, eds, *Public and private social policy: Health and pension policies in a new era*, 15–44. Basingstoke: Palgrave Macmillan.

Swank, Duane. 2002. *Global capital, political institutions, and policy change in developed welfare states*. Cambridge: Cambridge University Press.

Sykes, Gary, Barbara Schneider, and David N. Plank. eds 2009. *Handbook on education policy research*. New York: Routledge.

Taylor-Gooby, Peter, ed. 2004. *New risks, new welfare: The transformation of the European welfare state*. Oxford: Oxford University Press.

Teles, Steven M. 1998. "The dialectics of trust: Ideas, finance, and pension privatization in the US and the UK." Paper presented at the annual meeting of the Association for Public Policy Analysis and Management, New York, October.

Thelen, Kathleen. 2003. "How institutions evolve: Insights from comparative-historical analysis." In James Mahoney and Dietrich Rueschemeyer, eds, *Comparative-historical analysis: Innovations in theory and method*, 208–40. New York: Cambridge University Press.

Thelen, Kathleen. 2004. *How institutions evolve: The political economy of skills in Germany, Britain, the United States, and Japan*. New York: Cambridge University Press.

Théret, Bruno. 1999. "Regionalism and federalism: A comparative analysis of the regulation of economic tensions between regions by Canadian and American federal intergovernmental programmes." *International Journal of Urban and Regional Research* 23(3): 479–512.

Théret, Bruno. 2002. *Protection sociale et fédéralisme: L'Europe dans le miroir de l'Amérique du Nord*. Brussels: Peter Lang; Montreal: Presses de l'Université de Montréal.

Timonen, Virpi. 2003. *Restructuring the welfare state: Globalization and social policy reform in Finland and Sweden*. Cheltenham: Edward Elgar.

Titmuss, Richard M. 1963a. *Essays on "the welfare state"* (Second Edition). London: George Allen & Unwin.

Titmuss, Richard M. 1963b. "War and social policy." In *Essays on "the welfare state"* (Second Edition), 75–87. London: Unwin University Press.

References

Topalov, Christian. 2000. *Naissance du chômeur, 1880–1910*. Paris: Albin Michel.

Trattner, Walter I. 1998. *From poor law to welfare state: A history of social welfare in America* (Sixth Edition). New York: Free Press.

Trepagnier, Barbara. 2006. *Silent racism: How well-meaning white people perpetuate the racial divide*. Boulder, CO: Paradigm Publishers.

Turgeon, Lynn. 1996. *Bastard Keynesianism: The evolution of economic thinking and policymaking since World War II*. Westport, CT: Greenwood Press.

Turner, Bryan S. 1993. *Citizenship and social theory*. London: Sage.

Tynes, Sheryl R. 1996. *Turning points in Social Security: From "cruel hoax" to "sacred entitlement."* Palo Alto, CA: Stanford University Press.

United States House of Representatives. 2006. *The impact of President Bush's budget on veterans' health care in Massachusetts's 6th Congressional District*. Washington, DC: Committee on Government Reform, Minority Staff.

US Department of Housing and Urban Development. 2009. "Housing Choice Vouchers fact sheet." Washington, DC. http://www.hud.gov/offices/pih/programs/hcv/about/fact_sheet.cfm (accessed May 18, 2010).

Vaillancourt Rosenau, Pauline, ed. 2000. *Public–private policy partnerships*. Cambridge, MA: MIT Press.

Vale, Lawrence J. 2000. *From the Puritans to the projects: Public housing and public neighbors*. Cambridge, MA: Harvard University Press.

van Wormer, Katherine. 2006. *Introduction to social welfare and social work*. Belmont, CA: Wadsworth Publishing.

Veit-Wilson, John. 2000. "States of welfare: a conceptual challenge." *Social Policy & Administration* 34(1): 1–25.

Waddan, Alex. 2003. "Redesigning the welfare contract in theory and practice: Just what is going on in the USA?" *Journal of Social Policy* 32(1): 19–35.

Wall Street Journal. 2010. "What's in the Bill." March 22.

Wallerstein, Immanuel. 1974. *The modern world-system*. New York: Academic Press.

Walley, Tom, Alan Haycox, and Angela Boland. 2004. *Pharmacoeconomics*. New York: Elsevier.

Walsh, James I. 2000. "When do ideas matter? Explaining the successes and failures of Thatcherite ideas." *Comparative Political Studies* 33(4): 483–516.

Walters, William. 2000. *Unemployment and government: Genealogies of the social*. Cambridge: Cambridge University Press.

Washington Post. 2008. "The Wurzelbacher effect: Government has been spreading the wealth for many decades." *Washington Post*, November 2: B06.

Weaver, R. Kent. 1986. "The politics of blame avoidance." *Journal of Public Policy* 6(4): 146–61.

Weaver, R. Kent. 1988. *Automatic government: The politics of indexation*. Washington, DC: Brookings Institution Press.

Weaver, R. Kent. 2000. *Ending welfare as we know it.* Washington, DC: Brookings Institution Press.

Weaver, R. Kent. 2003. *The politics of public pension reform.* Working Paper 2003–06. Chestnut Hill, MA: Center for Retirement Research at Boston College.

Weber, Max. 1978. *Economy and society: An outline of interpretive sociology.* 2 vols. Berkeley: University of California Press.

Weber, Max. 2003. *The Protestant ethic and the spirit of capitalism.* Mineola, NY: Dover Publications.

Weir, Margaret. 1992. *Politics and jobs.* Princeton: Princeton University Press.

White, Joseph. 2001, *False alarm: Why the greatest threat to Social Security and Medicare is the campaign to "save" them.* Baltimore: Johns Hopkins University Press.

Wilensky, Harold L. 1975. *The welfare state and equality.* Berkeley: University of California Press.

Wilensky, Harold L. 2002. *Rich democracies: Political economy, public policy, and performance.* Berkeley: University of California Press.

Williamson, John, and Fred C. Pampel. 1993. *Old-age security in comparative perspective.* New York: Oxford University Press.

Wilton, Tamsin. 2000. *Sexualities in health and social care: A textbook.* Philadelphia: Open University Press.

Wincott, Daniel. 2001. "Reassessing the social foundations of welfare (state) regimes," *New Political Economy* 6(3): 409–25.

Wincott, Daniel. 2003. "Slippery concepts, shifting context: (national) states and welfare in the Veit-Wilson/Atherton debate," *Social Policy & Administration* 37(3): 305–15.

Winter, Ian. 1999. "Home ownership and social policy in an ageing society." *Family Matters* 52: 9–11.

Wiseman, Michael, and Martynas Yčas. 2008. "The Canadian safety net for the elderly." *Social Security Bulletin* 68(2): 53–67.

Woodall, Ann M. 2005. *What price the poor? William Booth, Karl Marx and the London residuum.* Aldershot: Ashgate.

World Bank. 1994. *Averting the old age crisis: Policies to protect the old and promote growth.* Washington, DC: The World Bank.

Yeates, Nicola. 2001. *Globalization and social policy.* London: Sage.

Zelizer, Julian E. 1998. *Taxing America: Wilbur D. Mills, Congress, and the state, 1945–1975.* New York: Cambridge University Press.

Zhang, Sheldon. 2007. *Smuggling and trafficking in human beings: All roads lead to America.* Westport, CT: Praeger.

Index

Note: page numbers in italics denote tables

185

Index

Baby Boomers 24, 32
Ball, Robert 78
bankruptcy 132
Barr, Nicholas 35
Bartels, Larry 139–40
Beehner, Lionel 148
Belgium
  health-care 36
  labor party 84
  old-age insurance 32–3
  secession threat 59
  social insurance 36, 70
  territorially divided 65
Bell, Daniel: *The Coming of the Post-Industrial Society* 121
Benson Gold, Rachel 147
Berkowitz, Edward D. 3, 81, 94–5
Beveridge, William 70, 77–8
Beveridge model 70–1
Bianchi, Suzanne M. 127
big government concept 95
"big picture" concept 2, 4, 6, 10, 100, 109, 152–4
Bismarck, Otto von 69, 70, 73
Blair, Tony 110, 117, 160n7
blame avoidance 100–1
Blank, Helen 42
Blau, Francine D. 138–9
blind pensions 72
Blyth, Mark 156
Bonoli, Giuliano 51, 123, 124, 128, 129, 130
Boschee, Marlys Ann 41
Brooks, Clem 87
Brown, Drusilla K. 145
Brown, Scott 135
bureaucracy 85, 97, 159n9
Bush, George W. 104, 112, 147
business community/federalism 74

California 40, 95–6
Campbell, John L. 149
Canada
  aboriginal peoples 53
  care-giving/gender 130
  decentralization of welfare state 61
  family allowance 26, 39

federal system 6, 30
French-/English-speaking 64
Guaranteed Income Supplement 21
health-care 23–4, 26, 35, 44, 88, 133, 157–8n6
health expenditure/GDP *133*
income tax *50*
labor party 84
as liberal welfare regime 5, 48, 55, 71
mothers in labor force 128
old-age insurance 81
Old Age Security 26
pharmaceutical industry 17
poverty 160n2
private benefits 16
private pensions 33, 54
Quebec 17, 41, 59, 64
social expenditure/GDP *50, 107*
social policy complexity 105
taxation 49
unemployment benefits 110
unemployment insurance 30, 81
universal programs 64, 133
Canada Health Act (1984) 158n6
capitalism
  class factors 12
  commodification of labor 14
  popular 96
  social policy 9–10, 15–16
  and state 54
care for elderly 104, 129–30
Casper, Lynne 127
Castel, Robert 11, 15–16, 22, 69
Castles, Francis G. 47, 60, 61, 150
CCF (Co-operative Commonwealth Federation) 84
charity boards 72
child-care
  affordable 127
  gender roles 39, 51
  private 42
  social-democratic regime 49
  subsidization 41, 42
  wage levels 125
  women in labor force 18, 41–2
Child Tax Credit (CTC) 39

Index

Index

Index

Index

Index